You can be eating until your heart's content. As long as you're starving on a nutritional basis your body is going to stay hungry to get those specific nutrients.

Jon Gabriel in 'Hungry for Change'.

WELCOME

I'm delighted you have chosen to purchase my delicious recipes using my favourite Food Heroes. Food Heroes, unlike super foods, are real whole foods and should be the main ingredient in all our meals. You will find more information about Food Heroes starting on page 119. If you want to find out why I turned to raw food, please read my story on page 134.

My intention for this book was to create a kind of workbook for your kitchen. A practical guide which is designed to help you develop your repertoire of raw food dishes and introduce you to some of the gems of raw food cuisine which delight my family, friends and guests at my raw food retreats and classes.

All recipes have been created to give you nutritional excellence for super immunity – to support your wellness and longevity. All recipes are also naturally free of gluten, dairy and refined sugar. In fact, I use natural sugars very sparingly, because while there are some healthier options to the refined, white stuff, any sugars become unhealthy if consumed in excess.

At the end of the book you find some references on where to source ingredients and where to learn more about the raw food lifestyle. Because once you start eating this way, you will undoubtedly want more.

Mostly, my aim is to inspire you with flavour ideas. And ultimately I want you to make up your own recipes. That's why I have added tips and variations to the recipes as well as space for you to make your own notes. So, for example, if you don't have yellow peppers but you have red ones, then make a note so you know whether you liked this variation of the recipe or not.

Let's get started!

FOREWORD

I trained with The Institute for Optimum Nutrition in London and have been practising in clinic as a Nutritional Therapist for the past 15 years. I came into using food as a therapy, not from the point of view of an already practising health professional, but as the owner of a small catering business and a lifelong love of good food.

In my practice I have found that the combination of investigating a patient's underlying biochemistry with the fun of planning new ways of eating has been both challenging and hugely rewarding. On the basis that every chemical reaction in our body, as well as the repair and formation of new cells is totally reliant on the nutrients absorbed from what we eat, there can be nothing more important than a healthy diet.

When Gabriela approached me with the idea of her raw food recipe book I was delighted to provide the nutritional profile for her chosen food heroes – a process that only served to reinforce my amazement at the healing power of food. Raw food is a wonderful way of providing true super-nutrition and while changing habits is not always easy, the health rewards of eating raw make it infinitely worthwhile.

Rowena Paxton

Rowena Paxton DipION CNHC
Member of the British Association for Applied Nutrition and Nutritional Therapy
CNHC Accredited
www.rowenapaxtonnutrition.com

FOOD HEROES

CONTENTS

WELCOME 1

FOREWORD 2

THANK YOU 7

WHY RAW FOOD 8

EQUIPMENT 9

START THE DAY 11
Pineapple Kale Smoothie 12
Tropical Green Smoothie 12
Berry Berry Smoothie 13
Super Green Smoothie 13
Cinnamon Buckwheat Crunch 15
Cacao Goji Buckwheat Crunch 16
Banana Breakfast Smoothie 17
Cacao Chia Pudding 18
Mulberry & Goji Berry Pudding 20
English Breakfast 21
Fruit & Greens Salad 23

BREAK FOR LUNCH 25
The Perfect Salad 26
Five-Minute Chop Bowl 27
Nori Rolls 28
Creamy Tomato & Red Pepper Soup 29
Carrot and Savoy Cabbage Salad 31
Mushroom & Basil Soup 32
Kelp Noodles with Spinach Pesto 33

Jewelled Broccoli Salad 34
Broad Bean Pâté 36
Sprouted Lentil Humus 37
Hungarian Cabbage Salad 38
Sprouted Quinoa Tabbouleh 39
Carrot & Beetroot Salad 41
Purple Sprouting in Tarragon Cream 42
Carrot Ginger Pâté 43

MEET TO EAT 45
Teriyake Noodles 46
Castara Sunset Noodles 48
Mushroom Steaks 49
Stuffed Portobello Mushrooms 51
Stuffed Tomatoes with Cheesy Sauce 53
Mini Peppers with Nut Cheese 54
Spicy Nori Bites 55
Thai Green Curry Kelp Noodles 56
Carrot Burgers 57
Courgette Ribbons with Smokey Tomato Sauce 58
Beetroot & Courgette Roulade 60
Spiced Red Cabbage 61
Nut 'Roast' 62
Rawsagne 64

CAKES & SWEETS 67
Lime Pie 68
Orange Cacao Torte 70

Cacao Nib Oat Bars 72

Apple Crumble 73

Banana Ice Cream 75

Macadamia Lemon Biscuits 76

Apple & Cranberry Oat Bar 77

Tahini Cacao Truffles 78

Incan Chocolate Torte 80

Raw Rocky Road 82

Black Forest Cherry Tumbler 83

Gooseberry Chia Mousse 84

Lemon Mango Cheese Cake 86

BREADS, CRACKERS & WRAPS 89

Moroccan Seed Crackers 90

Italian Seed Crackers 91

Rosemary & Beetroot Crackers 92

Yellow Pepper & Saffron Crackers 94

Garlic Croutons 95

Carrot and Onion Bread 97

Chia Seed Pizza Crust 98

Green Corn Wraps 100

Walnut & Raisin Bread 101

BASICS 103

Caramelised Onions 104

Date and Mulberry Paste 105

Marinated Mushrooms 106

Raw Tomato Chutney 107

Sprouted Buckwheat/Buckwheaties 108

Smoky Seeds 109

Spicy Curry Seeds 110

Nut 'Parmesan' 111

Pine Nut 'Parmesan' Flakes 112

Cranberry Relish 113

Hazelnut Milk 114

Cashew Cream 115

Cashew Yoghurt 116

Basic Macadamia Nut Cheese 117

Pickled Ginger 118

FOOD HEROES 119

Leafy Greens 120

Roots & Bulbs 121

Salads 123

Fruits 126

Herbs & Spices 129

Nuts & Seeds 131

Seagreens 133

Mushrooms 133

ABOUT GABRIELA LERNER 134

MORE RAW FOOD 136

INDEX 137

Piglet noticed that even though he had a very small heart, it could hold a rather large amount of gratitude.

A. A. Milne, Winnie The Pooh

THANK YOU!

Most of all I would like to thank you, my reader, for purchasing my first recipe book and for choosing to live a little in the raw. I created this book for you.

I would also like to thank my family for supporting me in this adventure, particularly my Mum, Erika, who always encourages me in whatever I choose to do in my life and who said to me, when I told her I would train in raw food, 'I always knew you would do something with food, just surprised you didn't do it much earlier'.

Also our daughters, Ira and Maria, who inspire me through living their lives exactly the way they want to. Thank you for your encouragement and enthusiasm.

A big thank you goes to my husband, Neil, whose photographs you will see throughout, who designed the layout and worked many hours to get the book print-ready. Thank you for keeping me focussed and helping me to get this book published. Thank you for believing in me. You're the pillar in my life. I love you.

Thank you to my friend, Rowena Paxton, who is an experienced nutritional therapist and whose knowledge and support have helped my own personal recovery from Fibromyalgia, Hypoglycemia and IBS. Rowena worked with me to develop the concept for this book and contributed the information on Food Heroes in the second part of the book.

Thank you also to my friend, Jane Etherton, who spent hours diligently editing the book with eagle eyes, sharp wit, a deep love for good food and a personal understanding of how to work with recipes.

There are many more people who have been instrumental in the making of this book. For example, my friend Fiona McInnes-Craig, who has pushed me to get it done. Thank you! And thanks to so many friends who have lent their support, tasted my food and given me feedback. You've all been behind the idea from the beginning, cheering me on as I created the recipes. You know who you are!

May your lives be filled with peace, love and nutritious food!

WHY RAW FOOD?

A vegetarian, live-food diet allows one to eat the least amount of food and receive the most nutritional and energetic impact.

Gabriel Cousens M.D.

There are a million and one books on the market about raw food and why it is good for us, some of which were written by raw food nutrition experts with 20 or 30 years experience. So you'll be happy to know that I'm going to keep this section short.

Raw food is live food. Enzymes, vitamins, phytonutrients and minerals are destroyed at temperatures above 46ºC (115ºF) and therefore most of these life-giving elements are lost in cooked food. Raw food is unprocessed and plant-based. It's a 'low footprint' food with the least pesticides or toxic contamination, particularly if you stick to mostly organic produce.

Contrary to popular belief, raw food, if prepared correctly, is actually easier to digest than cooked food and the body knows how to quickly utilise the nutrients without delay. Did you know that each plant comes with exactly the right enzymes to help you digest that particular food? This is an amazing design by nature, which we destroy through cooking.

Raw foods, eaten in a balanced way, are packed with nutrients and provide us with all we need: protein, carbohydrates, fat, minerals, vitamins and phytonutrients. There are only two vitamins that are hard to get through a raw, plant-based diet: vitamin B12 (many meat eaters also lack this essential vitamin) and vitamin D, which we get through sunshine. If you are concerned about these vitamins, you can get simple tests done through your doctor or online to check whether you need to supplement.

Raw food is delicious – once you develop a palate for it, you will no doubt want more of it. Once you start eating these clean, unprocessed and low sugar foods, you will soon start to feel more energy, be more closely connected to nature and more in tune with your body. Raw, plant-based, living food is not only beneficial for the body, spirit and the mind, but also for the environment. More people can be fed from an acre of vegetables than an acre of land dedicated to cattle or even an acre of wheat. Think about that.

To find out more about raw, plant-based, living food, I recommend you read Dr. Gabriel Cousens' '*Conscious Eating*' and '*Rainbow Green Live-Food Cuisine*' or Cherie Soria's '*Raw Food For Dummies*', to name just a few.

EQUIPMENT

Japanese chefs believe our soul goes into our knives once we start using them.

Masaharu Morimoto, Japanese chef

The two most import pieces of equipment are a good knife and a chopping board. A vegetable peeler is also helpful for peeling and slicing vegetables into ribbons. I find a nut milk bag quite essential for making nut milks, cheeses and for all sorts of tasks that require straining or draining. Once you know that raw food is for you, you may want to invest in equipment that makes your life easier and your food preparation faster.

Blenders

Consider a super fast blender, such as a Thermomix, Blendtec or Vitamix. High-speed blenders can create really smooth nut creams and smoothies; they blend faster, reducing oxidation and heat. Also useful is a mini blender like the Tribest Personal Blender, Nutribullet, or similar. These are great for one-person households, travel and making small batches, for example ground linseed or a quick salad dressing.

Food Processor

Unless you have a Thermomix, a food processor is helpful to chop nuts, make doughs and process foods coarsely. It can also help with slicing and grating large quantities.

Spiraliser

A spiraliser turns your favourite vegetable into noodles – just add a sauce of your choice.

Dehydrator

Many raw food recipes ask for a dehydrator. See my website for more information on how to choose the right one. In the meantime, you can dehydrate foods in your oven at low temperature, but long term that's not economical.

Juicer

There are no juicing recipes in this book though I personally juice daily. Once you start to get serious about raw food, you will probably want to get a good quality slow juicer.

Sprouting equipment

Sprouting equipment is not essential but can make sprouting seeds & legumes easier.

Check my website for more info: **www.radiantonraw.co.uk**

START THE DAY

Eat breakfast like a king, lunch like prince, and dinner like a pauper.

Adelle Davis, American Nutritionist

This well known and often mentioned quote by Adelle Davis, an American nutritionist and the author of books like 'Let's Eat Right to Keep Fit' and 'Let's Get Well' has a lot of truth to it. In our society, however, it is often difficult to stick to this rule for all three meals. I am nonetheless a great believer in a nutrition-rich breakfast that sets me up for the day ahead. I start mine with a green juice or smoothie and then follow it an hour or so later with a chia pudding or buckwheat crunch. This usually keeps me going well past lunch.

I recommend that you find your own eating rhythm. Try eating different foods and amounts at different times of the day and see how you feel half an hour later, an hour later, a few hours later. If, like me, you need to ensure you maintain your weight, then a smoothie followed by a dish containing some form of nuts and seeds may serve you well. If on the other hand you are trying to lose weight, then perhaps just 500ml (1 pint) of a green smoothie is all you need until lunch time, allowing your body to recognize the nutrition and burn some of the excess fat.

One thing's for sure though, you should not skip the early morning meal. It is called 'break-fast' for a reason. We break the fast after a night of not eating.

Many of my recipes use superfoods which add further nutrients. If you have any health concerns, please check with your doctor or health practitioner before using superfoods.

Maca: A Peruvian root that is rich in protein. It is known as an adaptogen and hormone balancer.

Lucuma: A Peruvian fruit powder with a subtle sweet flavour, rich in beta carotene.

Baobab: An African fruit powder, rich in fibre, vitamin C and calcium.

Mesquite: Also called Peruvian Carob, has a sweet, caramel flavour and is rich in protein.

Spirulina: A form of cyanobacterium high in protein, and containing all essential amino acids. It also contains vitamins, minerals and lipids such as GLA, ALA, EPA and DHA.

Chlorella: A single-cell freshwater green micro-algae which is nutrient dense and alkaline forming. A good source of protein, essential fatty acids, vitamins and minerals, chlorella is considered to be particularly helpful in removing toxins and heavy metals from the body.

PINEAPPLE KALE SMOOTHIE

Serves: 1-2
Equipment needed: blender

INGREDIENTS

4 kale leaves, hard stems removed, chopped

1 slice of fresh pineapple, peeled and chopped

½ banana, peeled and chopped

½ pear, core removed and chopped

½ lemon, juiced

200ml (¾ cup) water

Pineapple, banana and pear make this a great entry level smoothie. Over time, as your taste buds adjust to the green taste, it's a good idea to reduce the amount of sweet fruit and stick with more vegetables, as suggested in later recipes.

1. Blend all ingredients for 1-2 minutes until completely smooth.

> **TIP**
> Drink your smoothie as fresh as possible. But if time is an issue in the morning, I'd rather you prepared it the night before than not drink it at all. Keep it in the refrigerator and consume within 24 hours.

TROPICAL GREEN SMOOTHIE

Serves: 1-2
Equipment needed: blender

INGREDIENTS

2 large handfuls baby spinach

1 thick slice of pineapple (approx. 150g), peeled and chopped

½ ripe mango, peeled and chopped

1 blood orange, peeled

½ lemon, skin and pith

250ml unsweetened coconut water

In this smoothie I use the skin and pith of half a lemon. We so often have lemon skin left over from using lemon juice in recipes, yet there is a lot of goodness in the skin and the pith. It's rich in bioflavanoids and it gives this smoothie a slightly bitter taste.

1. Blend all ingredients for 1-2 minutes until completely smooth.

NOTES

FOOD HEROES
KALE
SPINACH
PINEAPPLE
MANGO

BERRY BERRY SMOOTHIE

Serves: 1-2
Equipment needed: blender

INGREDIENTS

1 romaine lettuce (also called cos), chopped

130g (1 cup) blueberries or blackberries

65g (½ cup) cranberries (fresh or frozen)

1 banana, peeled and chopped (optional)

½ orange, peeled and chopped

200ml (¾ cup) water or herbal tea

Berries are low sugar fruit, and cranberries are particularly sour. In this smoothie I've added a banana to make the smoothie sweeter. If you're ready to cut down on sweetness, try it first without the banana and then add banana bit by bit until you reach the sweetness that suits you best. The orange adds a little depth.

1. Blend all ingredients for 1-2 minutes until completely smooth.

SUPER GREEN SMOOTHIE

Serves: 1-2
Equipment needed: blender

INGREDIENTS

150ml green tea, cooled down a little

1 small bok choy, greens only, chopped

½ cucumber, chopped

1 celery stick, chopped

1 apple, chopped

½ lemon, chopped with peel

¼-1 teaspoon spirulina (optional)

¼ teaspoon chlorella (optional)

½ avocado, stone removed

Now we're getting a bit more serious with our smoothies. The avocado adds extra calories and good fats. Spirulina and chlorella give an extra energy boost and green tea adds antioxidants.

1. Blend the green tea, bok choi, cucumber, celery, apple, lemon, spirulina, chlorella and green tea for 1-2 minutes until completely smooth.
2. Scoop the avocado with a spoon out of its skin into the blender and blend until smooth.

TIP
Both spirulina and chlorella need a bit of getting used to. Therefore I recommend you start slowly with perhaps a 1/4 teaspoon of Spirulina first. Then build the quantity up over a period of time and eventually add the Chlorella.

NOTES

FOOD HEROES
BLUEBERRIES
CRANBERRIES
CELERY
GREENS

CINNAMON BUCKWHEAT CRUNCH

Serves: makes approx. 1 kg
Equipment needed: dehydrator
Plan ahead: needs pre-soaking and sprouting

INGREDIENTS

300g (2 cups) sprouted buckwheat (p. 108)

260g (2 cups) sunflower seeds, soaked 8-12 hours

280g (2 cups) of pumpkin seeds, soaked 8-12 hours

3 tablespoons lucuma or mesquite powder

2 tablespoons maca powder (optional)

3-5 teaspoons ground cinnamon

Granola is one of those convenient breakfast favourites, but most shop-bought granolas are full of grains and sugars. This crunch is grain free and subtly sweetened with maca and lucuma powder. It stores well and can be used as a dry 'trail-mix' type snack or just like granola by adding nut milk, cashew yoghurt or fruit.

1. Rinse and drain the seeds.
2. Mix all ingredients.
3. Spread thinly on a non stick dehydrator sheet and dehydrate 12-18 hours until crisp at no more than 46ºC (115ºF).
4. Leave the finished crunch to cool and then store in a jar.
5. Serve with your choice of nut milk, yoghurt, milk and/or fruit.

> **TIP**
> If you don't have a dehydrator you can also make this granola in the oven. Keep the temperature as low as your oven allows, ideally 50ºC or lower, with the door slightly open.

NOTES

FOOD HEROES
BUCKWHEAT SEEDS

CACAO GOJI BUCKWHEAT CRUNCH

A luxurious variation on the previous recipe using cacao and goji berries. The chia seeds add extra protein and omega 3 & 6 fatty acids, making this an excellent snack on the go.

Serves: makes approx. 1.1 kg
Equipment needed: dehydrator
Plan ahead: needs pre-soaking and sprouting

INGREDIENTS

100g (1 cup) goji berries

3 tablespoons chia seeds

240ml (1 cup) water

300g (2 cups) sprouted buckwheat (p.108)

260g (2 cups) sunflower seeds, soaked 8-12 hours

280g (2 cups) of pumpkin seeds, soaked 8-12 hours

100g (1 cup) cacao nibs

6 tablespoons raw cacao powder

3 tablespoons maca powder (optional)

2 tablespoons lucuma or mesquite powder

1. Soak the goji berries and chia seeds in 240ml water for 20 minutes. Stir occasionally.
2. Rinse and drain the sunflower, pumpkin seeds and buckwheat.
3. Combine the sprouted buckwheat, sunflower seeds, pumpkin seeds, goji berries and chia seeds with their soaking water.
4. Add the cacao nibs, cacao powder, maca and lucuma/mesquite powder, and mix well.
5. Spread in clusters on a non stick dehydrator sheet and dehydrate 12-18 hours until crisp at no more than 46ºC (115ºF).
6. Leave the finished crunch to cool and then store in a jar.
7. Serve with your choice of nut milk, yoghurt, milk and/or fruit or eat as a snack.

VARIATION

Use blueberries or raspberries from frozen instead of the goji berries. In this case only soak the chia seeds. Defrost and drain the berries and add them to the mix at step 3. Use the drained liquid from the berries in a smoothie.

NOTES

FOOD HEROES

BUCKWHEAT BERRIES

Serves: 1

Equipment needed: blender or mini-blender

INGREDIENTS

1 banana

125ml (½ cup) hazelnut milk (p.114)

1 tablespoon chia seeds

½ tablespoon maca powder (optional)

½ tablespoon hemp protein powder

1 teaspoon baobab powder

½ teaspoon cinnamon

a pinch ground cloves

BANANA BREAKFAST SMOOTHIE

This is my quick go-to breakfast when I've forgotten to soak chia seeds overnight. It's delicous and satisfying, with a lovely, creamy texture.

1. Blend all ingredients into a smooth cream.
2. Top with soaked nuts, seeds and dried fruit, such a goji or mulberries or pour onto buckwheat crunch (see pages 15 & 16).

TIP
If you don't have a blender, simply whisk all ingredients except the banana by hand and then pour it over a sliced banana.

VARIATIONS
Ripe pear, mango, orange and berries are all wonderful fruit to use instead of the banana. If you want to reduce your sugar intake, it's best to stick to berries.

NOTES

FOOD HEROES

**BANANA
HAZELNUTS
CHIA**

CACAO CHIA PUDDING

Serves: 1
Plan ahead: pre-soaking required the night before

INGREDIENTS

1 tablespoons chia seeds

1 tablespoons pumpkin seeds

125ml (½ cup) water

60ml (¼ cup) hazelnut milk (p.114)

1 tablespoons raw cacao powder

1 tablespoons shelled hemp seeds

½-1 tablespoons maca powder (optional)

½ teaspoon ground or freshly grated turmeric

1-2 tablespoons linseed, ground

Chia puddings are a wonderful nourishing and filling breakfast. With the added pumpkin and hemp seeds, this breakfast is rich in protein, minerals and essential Omega 3 & 6 oils.

1. Soak the chia seeds and pumpkin seeds in the 125ml (½ cup) water overnight.
2. Stir a couple of times in the first 10 minutes of soaking to distribute the chia seeds evenly.
3. In the morning add all the other ingredients into the pudding and stir well.
4. Serve with cashew yoghurt (page 116), soaked chopped nuts or fresh fruit.

TIP

If you're not used to maca powder start with a teaspoon and gradually increase the quantity day by day. To make warm chia pudding don't soak overnight, but mix all ingredients in the morning with hot (not boiling) water and leave for 15 minutes.

NOTES

FOOD HEROES

CHIA SEEDS
HEMP SEEDS
TURMERIC

MULBERRY & GOJI CHIA PUDDING

Serves: 1
Plan ahead: requires pre-soaking the night before

INGREDIENTS

1½ tablespoons chia seeds

1 tablespoon goji berries

1 tablespoon dried mulberries

125ml (½ cup) water

60ml (1/4 cup) hazelnut milk

1 tablespoon hemp powder

½-1 tablespoon baobab powder

1-3 tablespoons coconut oil, melted

2 tablespoons linseeds, freshly ground

Mulberries and goji berries are some of my favourite dried fruit. Together they make a powerful team. Goji berries, chia seeds and hemp powder are all high in protein – great to start the day!

1. Soak the chia seeds, goji berries and mulberries in the 125ml (½ cup) water overnight.
2. Stir a couple of times in the first 10 minutes of soaking to distribute the chia seeds evenly.
3. In the morning add all the other ingredients into the pudding and stir well. Serve with cashew yoghurt, chopped nuts or fruit.

VARIATIONS
Experiment with different flavours, spices and dried or fresh fruit to create your own favourite chia pudding. If you don't like it sweet, leave out the dry fruit and flavour with spices and cacao instead.

NOTES

FOOD HEROES
CHIA SEEDS
GOJI BERRIES
LINSEEDS

ENGLISH BREAKFAST

Serves: 2

Plan ahead: requires dehydrating, soaking and sprouting

INGREDIENTS

For the wilted spinach

150g baby spinach

2 teaspoons lemon juice

1 tablespoon olive oil

1 pinch sea salt

For the scrambled no-eggs

65g (½ cup) sunflower seeds

140g (½ cup) sprouted buckwheat (p.108)

65g (½ cup) Brazil nuts

1-2 tablespoons coconut oil

1 teaspoon dulse flakes

1 teaspoon turmeric

¼ teaspoon sea salt

125ml (½ cup) filtered water

Plus

6 slices Portobello mushroom steaks (p.49)

8 baby tomatoes, sliced

8 large basil leaves

4 raw crackers or 2 slices raw bread (p.89)

1 avocado, sliced

freshly ground pepper

Sometimes you just want something savoury for breakfast. This raw version of the English Breakfast combines bits from various recipes into a satisfying raw food morning meal.

1. Mix the baby spinach with the lemon juice, olive oil and sea salt and massage with your hands until it has a wilted, cooked appearance.
2. Divide the spinach between two large plates.
3. Place the sunflower seeds, buckwheat, Brazil nuts, dulse flakes, turmeric and water into a food processor and process until smooth.
4. Divide the 'scrambled no-eggs' between the two plates.
5. On each plate, layer half of the tomato slices with half of the basil leaves.
6. Add the slices of mushrooms and avocado.
7. Add two crackers or a slice of raw bread each.
8. Add freshly ground pepper to taste.

VARIATIONS

For the scrambled 'no-eggs' use sweetcorn (fresh or defrosted from frozen) instead of the buckwheat. Leave out the dulse and try some mustard.

NOTES

FOOD HEROES

SPINACH
DULSE
MUSHROOMS
TOMATO

FRUIT & GREEN SALAD

Serves: 2

INGREDIENTS

1 pear, cored and chopped

1 avocado, peeled and chopped

½ mango, peeled and chopped

½ pomegranate, seeds

8 strawberries, halved

3 sticks celery, chopped finely

55g (1 cup) chopped spinach leaves

½ lemon, juiced

I wasn't quite sure whether to put this recipe into the breakfast or lunch section of this book. It really works at any time of day. The spinach, celery and avocado turn a simple fruit salad into a substantial meal. This recipe is great as a take-away when travelling.

1. Combine all fruit and vegetables in a good sized bowl.
2. Pour the lemon juice over the fruit and vegetables, and mix carefully – avocado and mango can easily turn mushy, you want identifiable fruit pieces.

VARIATIONS

Try out different fruit combinations depending on season.

Mix some grated ginger into the lemon juice before pouring it over the fruit.

Top with Cinnamon Buckwheat Crunch (page 15) or Cacao Goji Buckwheat Crunch (page 16), or simply add some soaked and chopped seeds or nuts.

NOTES

**FOOD
HEROES**

**AVOCADO
SPINACH
CELERY
BERRIES**

BREAK FOR LUNCH

One cannot think well, love well, sleep well, if one has not dined well.

Virginia Woolf

We don't know what Virginia Woolf would have considered 'dining well'. She suffered from depression and there is now good evidence that a nutrition-rich diet can help with depression and mood swings and that a diet particularly rich in green vegetables can help reduce the risk of mental illnesses such as Alzheimer's and Dementia. Children are known to have conquered Attention Deficit Disorder and there are several case studies of people with bipolar conditions who have helped themselves through diet and no longer need medication. So while Virginia Woolf may not have been able to help her own mental wellness, she certainly had a point when she wrote this statement.

Eating meals rich in vegetables, fruit, nuts and seeds does help us to think well. My own experience is that when I changed my diet with a focus on nutritional excellence, it not only improved my physical health but I started to appreciate more, love more and sleep better.

So break for lunch, especially if your tendency is to work all through the day.

Here are some easy and fast recipes that can of course be enjoyed at any time of day, but that are particularly suitable for lunch, whether at home, at work or as a picnic on the beach. Most can be prepared the night before. Invest in a beautiful lunch box or tiffin box to take your home prepared raw food with you wherever you go.

Soaking nuts and seeds
Most nuts and seeds in my recipes are pre-soaked, from a few hours to overnight. Soaking them reduces natural enzyme inhibitors, phytic acid and oxalic acid so that they are easier to digest. Soaking also activates nuts or seeds – they 'spring into life' through the addition of water, thereby dramatically increasing their nutritional value. Always rinse and drain nuts and seeds after soaking and before using them in a recipe.

THE PERFECT SALAD

Serves: 1

INGREDIENTS

Basic dressing

½ lemon, juiced

1-3 tablespoon cold pressed olive oil

Freshly ground black pepper

Almond butter dressing

1 tablespoon almond butter

1 tablespoon cold pressed hemp seed oil

1 teaspoon raw cider vinegar

1 teaspoon chopped fresh herbs

Freshly ground black pepper and sea salt to taste

Avocado basil dressing

½ avocado, peeled and chopped

½ lime, juiced

2 tablespoons water

5 large basil leaves, chopped

Freshly ground black pepper and sea salt to taste

Most often my main meal of the day is a huge salad. And it never gets boring. It looks and tastes different every day and I always look forward to another plate of colourful and fresh goodness. Here's how to make the perfect, nutrition rich salad.

1. Cover a dinner plate with leafy greens, such as salad leaves, baby spinach, swiss chard, fresh herbs, watercress, baby kale and dandelion.
2. Add sliced or chopped vegetables depending on what's seasonally available, such as tomatoes, cucumber, celery, raddish, aspargus, carrot, beetroot, red or white cabbage.
3. Perhaps a tablespoon of fermeted vegetables would be nice. Try sauerkraut or kimchi, or a fermented nut cheese (page 117).
4. Sprinkle with a few sunflower shoots, alfalfa or sprouted lentils.
5. Add some seaweed in the form of dulse or nori flakes.
6. Marinated mushrooms (page 106) and smoky or spicy curry seeds (pages 109-110) will add flavour and protein.
7. Top it with sliced avocado, unless you use the avocado dressing.
8. Now mix or blend the dressing ingredients of your choice and pour over your salad.
9. Serve it with a cracker or a slice of raw carrot and onion bread (page 97).

NOTES

FOOD HEROES

LEAFY GREENS
ROOT VEGETABLES
AVOCADO
SEEDS

FIVE-MINUTE CHOP BOWL

Serves: 1-2

INGREDIENTS

¼ red cabbage, sliced thinly and discard tough bits

1 large handfull of kale, stems removed and chopped into thin strips

3 or 4 florettes of broccoli, sliced thinly

½ red pepper, sliced thinly

a sprinkle of sea salt

½ avocado, peeled and chopped

½ lemon, juiced

½ tablespoon extra virgin olive oil

Toppings

1 tablespoon sprouted lentils

1 tablespoon shelled hemp seeds

For a quick lunch I often just look in the refrigerator, grab a few vegetables chop them up and drizzle them with lemon juice and olive oil. My Five-Minute Chop Bowl is exactly that. Make it once following the recipe and you will know how to create your own variation with whatever is available. Filling, nutritious and yummy!

1. Mix the red cabbage, kale, broccoli and red pepper in a bowl and sprinkle with the sea salt.
2. Massage the vegetables with your hands to soften them until the red cabbage and kale wilt a little.
3. Add the avocado, lemon juice and olive oil and mix gently.
4. Top with sprouted lentils and shelled help seeds.

> **VARIATION**
> Add olives, nuts or seeds as a topping.

> **TIP**
> The secret to success with this salad is to cut the vegetables really thin! You don't want big chunks. Use a sharp knife or a vegetable slicer.

NOTES

FOOD HEROES

**KALE/CABBAGE
BROCCOLI
AVOCADO
PEPPERS**

NORI ROLLS

Serves: 2 for lunch
Equipment needed: food processor, bamboo sushi mat (optional)

INGREDIENTS

For the rice

1 parsnip, chopped

½ cauliflower, leaves and hard stems removed

60g (½ cup) macadamia nuts

60g (½ cup) pine kernels

1 tablespoon date & mulberry paste (p.105)

1 tablespoon raw apple cider vinegar

For the rolls

4 nori sheets

4 brown mushrooms, sliced thinly

½ lemon, juiced

1 carrot, julienned

1 ripe avocado, peeled and sliced

1 tablespoon sprouted sunflower shoots

1 tablespoon shelled hemp seed

4 sprigs watercress

In this recipe, the rice of a traditional sushi maki roll is replaced with parsnip & cauliflower rice. In our house this is what I make when we go for a picnic on the beach or when I need to feed us on a long-distance flight. They also make great party food.

1. Pulse all ingredients for the 'rice' a few seconds into a rice kernel consistency.
2. Lay a sheet of nori, shiny side down, on your sushi mat.
3. Spread a thin layer of 'rice' onto the sheet leaving the top 1/4 of the nori sheet empty.
4. Now lay the ingredients along a line in the middle of the rice.
5. Roll up the sheet tightly, tucking in the vegetables as you roll.
6. Use a little bit of clean water on the edge to stick the roll together and lay it on the seam.
7. Once all sheets have been rolled up, simply cut them in half and eat like a wrap.
8. Alternatively you can cut them into bite-size chunks like traditional sushi.
9. Serve with Tamari and pickled ginger (see page 118).

VARIATIONS

If you don't have time to make the rice, simply roll up the nori sheets with whatever vegetables you like. Moisten the end of the nori sheet with water to make it stick. Avocado or Cashew Yoghurt (page 116) is nice to add moisture.

NOTES

FOOD HEROES

MUSHROOMS
NORI
AVOCADO
WATERCRESS

CREAMY TOMATO & RED PEPPER SOUP

Serves: 2 for main course or 4 as a starter
Equipment needed: blender

INGREDIENTS

65g (½ cup) cashew nuts, soaked for 20 minutes

4 tomatoes, chopped

3 sun-dried tomatoes, soaked for 2 hours

1 red pepper, de-seeded and chopped

½ cup of water

1 date

1 tablespoon balsamic vinegar

¼ teaspoon sea salt

2 tablespoon extra virgin olive oil

1 tablespoon chopped basil

I liked the idea of creating a creamy soup and this is achieved by blending in cashew nuts, which also adds a bit of protein and good oils. On cold days it's lovely served warm!

1. Place the cashew nuts, tomatoes, sun-dried tomatoes, red pepper, water, date and balsamic vinegar into a blender.
2. Blend until smooth and creamy.
3. (Optional) Gently warm the soup to no more than 46ºC (115ºF).
4. Stir the olive oil into the soup.
5. Top the soup with the chopped basil and serve.

TIP
If you have a high speed blender or Thermomix, you can leave the skin on the tomatoes. However, if your blender isn't quite strong enough you might want to remove the skin to avoid bits in your soup. Place the tomatoes in a bowl and pour boiling water over them. Leave to sit for 5-10 minutes. The skins will now come off easily.

VARIATION
Add a dash of cayenne pepper or chilli for an extra kick.

NOTES

FOOD HEROES

RED PEPPER
TOMATOES
BASIL

CARROT & SAVOY CABBAGE SALAD

Serves: 2 for main course or 4 as a starter

INGREDIENTS

¼ savoy cabbage, sliced thinly

¼ teaspoon sea salt

3 carrots

3 tablespoons extra virgin olive oil

1 tablespoon apple cider vinegar

1 teaspoon coconut sugar (optional)

1 teaspoon ground coriander

freshly ground black pepper to taste

2 tablespoons black or white sesame seeds

2 tablespoons chopped fresh coriander

1 handful white or red organic grapes, sliced in half

Most green vegetables have quite a strong flavour, so here is a recipe that combines sweet savoy cabbage, carrot and grapes for a mild and fruity salad.

1. Mix the sliced cabbage with ¼ teaspoon sea salt.
2. Massage the cabbage with your hands until it starts to wilt and liquid is released.
3. Set aside and leave to marinate for 15 minutes.
4. Meanwhile grate the carrots on the side of the grater with the large holes.
5. Combine the oilve oil, cider vinegar, coconut sugar and ground coriander into a dressing and pour it over the carrots.
6. Squeeze as much liquid as possible out of the cabbage. This is best done by squeezing portions of the cabbage between two hands.
7. Add each portion of squeezed cabbage to the carrots.
8. Add the sesame seeds, chopped coriander and grapes and mix well.

> **VARIATION**
> I only ever use organic grapes. Non-organic grapes are heavily sprayed. If you can't get organic grapes, you can substitute with orange or mango slices.

NOTES

**FOOD
HEROES**
CABBAGE
CARROTS
GRAPES

MUSHROOM & BASIL SOUP

Serves: 2 for main course or 4 as a starter
Equipment needed: blender

INGREDIENTS

250g (3 cups) mushrooms

60g (¼ cup) raw white almond butter

2 tablespoons Tamari

½ lemon, juiced

1 garlic clove

250ml (1 cup) warm or cold water

2 tablespoons chopped basil

sea salt and black pepper to taste

Mushrooms, almonds and basil make a divine combination of flavours. A lovely soup served ice cold in the summer or slightly warmed in the winter.

1. Clean the mushrooms if necessary with a piece of kitchen towel.
2. Slice 4 mushrooms thinly and set aside.
3. Blend the remaining mushrooms with the almond butter, Tamari, lemon juice, garlic and water into a smooth soup.
4. Add more water if necessary.
5. Add the basil to the soup and blend again briefly.
6. Season with salt and pepper.
7. Pour into individual soup bowls and sprinkle with the previously reserved, sliced mushrooms.

TIP
Are mushrooms safe to eat raw? Raw mushrooms contain small amounts of agaritine which can be toxic if eaten in large amounts. Cooking or storing them in the refrigerator breaks down the argaritine. There are enough experts who believe eating them raw in moderate amounts is completely safe. If you feel uncomfortable eating them raw, simply heat the soup to around 60°C after blending.

NOTES

FOOD HEROES
MUSHROOMS
GARLIC
BASIL

KELP NOODLES WITH SPINACH PESTO

Serves: 4
Equipment needed: food processor or blender
Plan ahead: requires pre-soaking

INGREDIENTS

350g (12oz) kelp noodles

50g (1 packed cup) baby spinach, chopped roughly

1 bunch fresh basil, chopped roughly

65g (½ cup) macadamia nuts

1-3 garlic cloves, chopped into quarters

3 tablespoons extra virgin olive oil

2 tablespoons nutritional yeast flakes (optional)

2 teaspoons apple cider vinegar

¼ teaspoon sea salt

50g (½ cup) pecan nuts, pre-soaked for 8-12 hours

Kelp noodles are the 'fast food' noodles in the raw food kitchen. Packed full of minerals, they are virtually calorie free and don't have a flavour. They really are a carrier for great sauces.

1. Soak the kelp noodles in cold water for 20-30 minutes.
2. In the meantime add the baby spinach, basil, macadamia nuts, garlic cloves, olive oil, nutritional yeast flakes, cider vinegar and sea salt to a food processor or blender and process into a paste.
3. Rinse and drain the pecan nuts.
4. Add them to the pesto and pulse a couple of times to blend into the pesto but still keep some crunch.
5. Rinse and drain the kelp noodles.
6. Cut the noodles with scissors into smaller pieces.
7. In a large bowl mix the kelp noodles and pesto with your hands.
8. Leave to marinate for at least 15 minutes or overnight.

VARIATION
Instead of kelp noodles you can use spiralised courgette.

TIP
The pesto can be stored in an airtight glass jar in the refrigerator for up to two weeks. It also makes a delicious stuffing for baby vegetables such as button mushrooms, baby tomatoes or mini peppers.

NOTES

FOOD HEROES
KELP
SPINACH
GARLIC

JEWELLED BROCCOLI SALAD

Serves: 2 for main course, 4 as a starter
Plan ahead: requires pre-soaking

INGREDIENTS

For the dressing

1 lemon, juiced

6 tablespoons cold pressed or roasted pumpkin seed oil

1 tablespoon freshly grated ginger

2 teaspoons coconut sugar

¼ teaspoon sea salt

freshly ground pepper to taste

For the salad

1 small head of broccoli, hard stem removed and sliced thinly

1 courgette, sliced into batons

1 pomegranate, seeds only

50g (½ cup) walnuts, pre-soaked for 8-12 hours

Austria is the capital of pumpkin seed oil and this recipe was developed when I stayed there visiting my parents. The juicy and sweet pomegranate seed complements the green vegetables well and makes this dish look luxurious.

1. Combine all ingredients for the dressing and mix well.
2. Place the sliced broccoli and courgette batons into a large bowl.
3. Pour the dressing over the vegetables and mix well by hand, massaging the dressing gently into the vegetables to soften them slightly.
4. Leave to marinate for 10-15 minutes.
5. Rinse and drain the walnuts and mix them with the pomegranate seeds into the salad.

> **TIP**
> I like making the dressing for this salad in my mini-blender because it emulsifies the oil with the rest of the ingredients. If you have a mini blender, then you don't need to peel or grate the ginger either. Just throw it all into the blender and blend away.

> **VARIATIONS**
> Pomegranates are not always available. Try blood oranges or strawberries instead. Use pecan nuts instead of walnuts.

NOTES

FOOD HEROES
BROCCOLI
POMEGRANATE
WALNUTS

Equipment needed: Food Processor

INGREDIENTS

500g (1lb) fresh broad beans

1 garlic clove, chopped into quarters

30g (¼ cup) pine nuts

2 tablespoons nutritional yeast flakes

4 tablespoons extra virgin olive oil

½ lemon, juiced

2 pinches sea salt

1 tablespoon chopped parsley

BROAD BEAN PÂTÉ

Enjoy this simple but protein rich pâté with crudités or raw crackers. It is also nice as a filling for salad or cabbage wraps.

1. Remove the broad beans from their pods.
2. Place them into a bowl and pour hot (just off the boil) water over them.
3. Soak for 2-3 minutes and then pop the beans out of their tough outer skins.
4. Place the skinned beans, garlic, pine nuts, yeast flakes, olive oil, lemon juice and sea salt into a food processor and pulse several times to create a pâté.
5. Sprinkle with the chopped parsley.

> **TIP**
> Choose young broad beans, alternatively try this recipe with fresh or frozen peas (use roughly 200g). Sprinkle with chopped mint.

NOTES

FOOD HEROES

BEANS
PARSLEY

Equipment needed: food processor

INGREDIENTS

300g (3 cups) sprouted brown or green lentils

100g raw almond butter

70g raw tahini (sesame butter)

2 garlic cloves, chopped into quarters

3 tablespoons unpasteurised miso

3 tablespoons extra virgin olive oil

1 tablespoon lemon juice

½ tablespoon apple cider vinegar

1 teaspoon ground cumin

2 tablespoons chopped parsley

1 tablespoon black sesame seed (optional)

SPROUTED LENTIL HUMMUS

This is another delicious protein-rich pâté and a great way to eat sprouted lentils. Try it with crackers or a slice of Carrot & Onion Bread (page 97).

1. Place the sprouted lentils, almond butter, tahini, garlic, Tamari, olive oil, lemon juice, apple cider vinegar and ground cumin into a food processor.
2. Process into a smooth hummus consistency.
3. Add the chopped parsley and mix it into the hummus.
4. Decorate with black sesame seed or more chopped parsley.

> **TIP**
> Lentils are easy to sprout. Although I mostly buy my sprouting seeds from a specialist supplier, I have had good results with organic lentils from the supermarket. Soak them in water overnight. The next day, rinse and drain them. Keep them in a glass jar and rinse and drain every 12 hours until tiny tails emerge. Don't let the tail grow larger than the lentil, as this makes the sprouts bitter.

NOTES

FOOD HEROES
LENTILS
SESAME SEEDS

HUNGARIAN CABBAGE SALAD

Serves: 4

Equipment needed: food processor (optional for slicing the cabbage)

INGREDIENTS

1 white cabbage

2 teaspoons sea salt

2 tablespoons apple cider vinegar

2 tablespoons extra virgin olive oil

2 teaspoons coconut sugar or nectar

2 teaspoons caraway seeds

freshly ground black pepper to taste

In Hungary and Austria this is a popular salad that is usually made with a significant amount of sugar. I've replaced the sugar in this recipe with coconut sugar, but you could also use a small amount of agave syrup or honey.

1. Remove the outer leaves of the cabbage, quarter it and remove the hard core.
2. Slice the cabbage as thinly as you can either by using a food processor, mandolin or a large, sharp knife.
3. Sprinkle the sea salt onto the cabbage and massage it with your hands until the cabbage starts to wilt and draws moisture.
4. Leave to marinate for 15-20 minutes.
5. Taste the cabbage to check the saltiness. If it's too salty, then rinse the cabbage in water before proceeding to step 6.
6. Now squeeze as much liquid as you can from the cabbage. Do this by taking a handful of cabbage and squeezing it between your hands. Once squeezed transfer it to a fresh bowl.
7. Repeat step 6 until all of the cabbage has been squeezed.
8. Add the cider vinegar, olive oil, coconut sugar and caraway seeds and mix well.
9. Leave to stand for a further 10-15 minutes to allow the flavours to develop. Add freshly ground black pepper to taste.

> **TIP**
> Use this salad sprinkled over mixed green salads or in food wraps. It will store in the refrigerator for one week. Try different seeds instead of the caraway, such as cumin or coriander.

NOTES

FOOD HEROES
CABBAGE

SPROUTED QUINOA 'TABBOULEH'

Serves: 2 for main course or 4 as a starter
Equipment needed: sprouting jar (optional)
Plan ahead: requires pre-soaking and sprouting

INGREDIENTS

2 leaves Swiss chard, stems removed

30g (¼ cup) raisins, soaked for 2 hours

130g (1 cup) white or black quinoa, sprouted

1 carrot, finely cubed

1 tomato, finely chopped

65g (½ cup) peas, fresh or from frozen

1 spring onion, sliced finely

1 bunch fresh coriander, chopped

3 twigs mint, chopped

3 tablespoons apple cider vinegar

1-3 tablespoons extra virgin olive oil

1 tablespoon unpasteurised miso

1-2 teaspoons soaking liquid from the raisins

30g (¼ cup) black sesame seeds

In this recipe the sprouted quinoa replaces the bulgur or couscous that we usually associate with tabbouleh. Serve it with a generous portion of mixed green leaves.

1. Roll the leaves of the Swiss chard lengthwise and then slice them into very thin ribbons with a sharp knife.
2. Drain the raisins but reserve the liquid for sweetening.
3. Mix the chard with the sprouted quinoa, carrot, tomato, peas, raisins, spring onion, coriander and mint.
4. Mix the cider vinegar, olive oil and miso into a dressing and add 1-2 teaspoons of the soaking liquid from the raisins to achieve a sweetness to your liking.
5. Pour the dressing over the vegetables and mix well.
6. Sprinkle with black sesame seeds.

VARIATION

You can use cooked quinoa instead of sprouted quinoa, but I recommend you stay away from wheat based 'empty calories' such as couscous.

TIP

Sprouting quinoa. Soak white or black quinoa in water overnight. The next morning, rinse and drain the quinoa. Leave in a jar for 24-48 hours, rinsing twice a day with fresh water, until small tails emerge. Ensure you drain the quinoa well after each rinse. Once sprouted it will keep in the refrigerator for 2-3 days.

NOTES

FOOD HEROES

HERBS
CARROT
LEAFY GREENS

CARROT & BEETROOT SALAD

Serves: 2 for main course or 4 as a starter
Equipment needed: grater or food processor

INGREDIENTS

3 small carrots

1 medium beetroot

2.5cm (1") fresh ginger, grated

2 tablespoons lemon juice

½ tablespoon raw apple cider vinegar

½ tablespoon Tamari

2 teaspoons date & mulberry paste (p.105)

2 tablespoons extra virgin olive oil

2 tablespoons raw extra virgin sesame oil

2 tablespoons chopped, fresh coriander

2 tablespoons sesame seeds

This simple but beautiful recipe never fails to impress with its intense colours and gingery flavours. Serve it on a bed of lambs lettuce or baby spinach.

1. Grate the carrots and beetroot on the large side of a hand grater.
2. Mix the ginger, lemon juice, cider vinegar, Tamari, date & mulberry paste, olive oil and sesame oil with the vegetables and leave to marinate for 15-30 minutes.
3. Add the chopped coriander and sesame seeds before serving.

VARIATION
Don't like beetroot? They are so good for you, but if you must you can make this salad just with carrots.

TIP
This dish can be made much faster by processing it in a food processor or Thermomix. Chop the carrot and beetroot into chunks, place with all the other ingredients into the food processor and pulse a few times to get a grated consistency.

NOTES

FOOD HEROES

CARROT
BEETROOT
GINGER

PURPLE SPROUTING BROCCOLI WITH TARRAGON CREAM

Serves: 2-4
Equipment needed: blender
Plan ahead: requires pre-soaking

INGREDIENTS

500g (1lb) purple sprouting broccoli, sliced thinly
½ lemon, juiced
¼ teaspoon sea salt

For the cream

65g (½ cup) cashew nuts, soaked for 30 minutes
65g (½ cup) sunflower seeds, soaked for 30 minutes
70g (½ cup) macadamia nuts, soaked for 30 minutes
1 lemon, zest and juice
2 tablespoons extra virgin olive oil
¼-½ teaspoon sea salt
2 tablespoons nutritional yeast flakes (optional)
240ml (1 cup) water
2 tablespoons chopped, fresh tarragon
8 black olives, sliced
½ preserved lemon, finely chopped

After a long winter finding the first purple sprouting broccoli at the local market is always a delight and a sign that spring is truly on its way. Served with this subtly flavoured cream it makes a luxurious side dish or main course.

1. Mix the purple sprouting broccoli slices with the lemon juice and sea salt.
2. Massage the vegetables gently and leave to marinate while you prepare the cream.
3. Rinse and drain the cashew nuts, sunflower seeds and macadamia nuts.
4. Combine the nuts with the lemon zest & juice, olive oil, sea salt, yeast flakes and water in a blender and blend at high speed for up to 2 minutes to create a smooth cream.
5. Add the chopped tarragon and mix again briefly.
6. Pour the cream over the purple sprouting broccoli and mix well.
7. Add the olives and preserved lemon and mix again.

TIP

You can buy raw preserved lemons or you can make your own from lemons you've squeezed for other recipes. Pack 8 squueezed lemon halves into a jar with a tight fitting lid, mix 2 teaspoons of sea salt in hot (not boiling) water. Add some coriander and cumin seed to the jar and pour the salt water over the lemons. Make sure they are covered by liquid. Leave in a cool dark place for 4-6 weeks. Once opened, store them in the refrigerator. If you don't use them often, freeze them in portions.

NOTES

FOOD HEROES
PURPLE SPROUTING BROCCOLI
LEMONS
PARSLEY

CARROT & GINGER PÂTÉ

Serves: 2 for main course or 4 as a starter
Equipment needed: food processor
Plan ahead: requires pre-soaking

INGREDIENTS

250g (4-5) carrots, chopped

65g (½ cup) sunflower seeds, soaked for 8-12 hours

1 celery stick, chopped

2.5-4cm (1"-1½") fresh ginger, grated

1 tablespoon raisins

2 tablespoons orange juice

2 tablespoon unpasteurised miso

1 shallot or spring onion, chopped

1 tablespoon chopped coriander

70g (½ cup) almonds, soaked for 8-12 hours and finely chopped

black pepper to taste

The carrots, raisins and ginger in this pâté make this a delicious spread for a cracker or wrapped up in a cabbage or lettuce leaf.

1. Place all ingredients except the chopped coriander, chopped almonds and black pepper into a food processor and process into a pâté.
2. Stir the coriander and almonds into the pâté by hand and season with black pepper.

> **TIP**
> This dish will store in the refrigerator for 2-3 days. Alternatively freeze any left-overs in portions. Defrost for 2 hours and serve with crackers, raw bread or crudités. Top with sprouts or microgreens.

NOTES

FOOD HEROES

CARROT
CELERY
CORIANDER

MEET TO EAT

Making raw food for friends and family is a wonderfully rewarding activity. It never ceases to amaze me how nobody ever declines a well made raw dish. The beauty of the fresh ingredients and abundance of the avours, and the satisfying but light feeling after the meal, make raw food ideal for entertaining. Not to mention of course that most things can be prepared in advance, leaving the 'cook' free to enjoy the company of their guests rather than slaving over a hot stove.

Here are my favourite recipes for entertaining. I usually serve these for dinner at my retreats. At these times the idea of eating 'like a pauper' goes right out the window. However, keep in mind that raw food is always a light affair. Some raw food experts say you can't over-eat on raw food. I'm not sure about that, but what I do know is that it won't hang around for long, burdening your digestive system. Instead it will keep you feeling well, satisfied and nourished.

The recipes in this section take a little more preparation. Most can be prepared ahead of time and kept in the refrigerator for a couple of days or be frozen. There are also a few appetizer or canapé recipes that will be perfect for a party.

If the divine creator has taken pains to give us delicious and exquisite things to eat, the least we can do is prepare them well and serve them with ceremony.

Fernand Point, French chef, restaurateur and father of modern 'French cuisine'.

TERIYAKI NOODLES

Fast and easy to make, teriyake noodles make a satisfying lunch or dinner dish.

Serves: 2 as a main course or 4 as a starter
Equipment needed: spiraliser, mini blender (optional)
Plan ahead: requires pre-soaking

INGREDIENTS

For the noodles

2 thick carrots, spiralised

1 medium courgette, spiralised

1 fennel bulb, sliced thinly

100g (1 cup) bean sprouts

20g (½ cup) Hijiki seaweed, soaked for 15 minutes

30g (¼ cup) sesame seeds

For the marinade

125ml (½ cup) cold pressed sesame oil

60ml (¼ cup) Tamari

2 tablespoons Japanese rice vinegar

1 tablespoon coconut sugar

1 garlic clove

2.5cm (1") fresh ginger, grated

Pickled Ginger to garnish (p.118)

1. Combine the spiralised carrots, courgette and fennel bulb with the bean sprouts.
2. Mix all ingredients for the marinade and add to the vegetables.
3. Mix well and leave to marinate for 30 minutes or longer.
4. Rinse and drain the seaweed and add to the vegetables.
5. Add the sesame seeds and gently mix the seaweed and seeds into the vegetables.

VARIATIONS
Try spiralising other vegetables, such as beetroot, squash, celeriac or turnip.
Use Arame seaweed instead of Hijiki or simply sprinkle the finished dish with Nori or Dulse akes.

TIPS
Instead of spiralising the carrot and courgette, they can also be sliced into ribbons with a vegetable peeler.

NOTES

FOOD HEROES
CARROTS
FENNEL
SEAWEEDS
GINGER

CASTARA SUNSET NOODLES

Serves: 2 as a main course or 4 as a starter
Equipment needed: spiraliser, mini blender

INGREDIENTS

For the noodles

2 carrots, spiralised

1 sweet potato, peeled and spiralised

1 large parsnip, spiralised

½ cabbage, outer leaves & hard core removed, thinly sliced

½ fennel, thinly sliced

1 small papaya, peeled, de-seeded & sliced. Reserve the seeds for the dressing

2 spring onions, chopped

1 tablespoon black sesame seeds

For the marinade

60ml (¼ cup) Tamari

60 ml (¼ cup) raw cold pressed sesame oil

60 ml (¼ cup) roasted sesame oil (not raw)

2 limes, juice and zest

½ lemon, juiced

1 teaspoon cider vinegar

2 dates, pitted and chopped

1 garlic clove, crushed

1 tablespoon freshly grated ginger

2 teaspoons fresh papaya seeds

1 teaspoon fresh turmeric, grated or ground turmeric

½ teaspoon mixed spice or allspice

½ teaspoon cinnamon

1 dash of cayenne

fresh coriander and basil for decoration

This is a variation of the Teriyake Noodle recipe on page 46. The flavours were inspired by my stay on Tobago at Castara Retreats, where the sunset saturates everything with a wonderful golden glow that is represented in this dish. It has a lot of ingredients but it's worth the effort!

1. Mix the carrot, sweet potato, parsnip, cabbage and fennel in a large bowl.
2. Make the marinade by blending all ingredients until smooth and emulsified.
3. Add the dressing to the vegetables and mix well with your hands.
4. Leave to marinate for 15-20 minutes.
5. Add the papaya, spring onions and black sesame seeds and gently mix again.
6. Serve with a sprinkle of chopped herbs and extra sesame seeds.

> **VARIATIONS**
> Try spiralising other vegetables, such as beetroot, squash, celeriac or turnip.

NOTES

FOOD HEROES
ROOT VEGETABLES

MUSHROOM STEAKS

Serves: 4-6
Equipment needed: dehydrator or oven
Plan ahead: requires dehydrating

INGREDIENTS

4-6 large portobello mushrooms

1 lemon, zest and juice

1 garlic clove, crushed

4 tablespoons extra virgin olive oil

2 tablespoons chopped parsley

These mushroom steaks are quick to make in either a dehydrator or oven. Serve them with sour cream (page 52), cranberry relish (page 113), spiced red cabbage (page 61) and a large mixed green salad.

1. Clean the mushrooms if necessary and remove the stems.
2. Slice the mushrooms 2cm (3/4") thick.
3. Mix the lemon juice with the lemon zest, garlic, olive oil and parsley and pour over the mushroom slices.
4. Gently turn the mushrooms in the marinade. This is best done by hand.
5. After 30 minutes remove the mushroom steaks from the marinade and place them onto a non-stick dehydrator sheet.
6. Dehydrate the mushrooms for one hour at 52°C (125°F).
7. Reduce the heat to 46°C (115°F) and dehydrate for a further 4-6 hours depending on the desired softness. I like mine soft but juicy.

TIP
If you don't have a dehydrator, you can warm the mushrooms through in the oven at the lowest temperature setting but reduce the time to one or two hours and check regularly. Dehydrated mushrooms will keep in the refrigerator for 3-4 days.

NOTES

FOOD HEROES

MUSHROOMS
GARLIC
PARSLEY

STUFFED PORTOBELLO MUSHROOMS WITH HERB SOUR CREAM

Serves: 4

Equipment needed: food processor, dehydrator (optional)

Plan ahead: requires pre-soaking and dehydrating

INGREDIENTS

For the mushrooms

4 extra large portobello mushrooms

½ lemon, zest and juice

¼ teaspoon sea salt

3 tablespoons extra virgin olive oil

For the stuffing

50g (½ cup) walnuts, soaked for 8-12 hours

1 tablespoon sesame seeds

6 sun-dried tomatoes, soaked for 2 hours

1 tablespoon goji berries, soaked for 2 hour

½ lemon, zest and juice

130g (1 cup) sprouted or cooked quinoa

2 tablespoons chopped parsley

Sea salt and black pepper to taste

FOOD HEROES

MUSHROOMS
WALNUTS
PARSLEY
LEMON

Portobello mushrooms make an impressive dish to serve your guests. It is best served with a large mixed green salad, simply dressed with lemon juice and olive oil. I prefer serving the mushrooms slightly warm straight from the dehydrator onto pre-warmed plates.

Marinating the mushrooms

1. Clean the mushrooms if necessary and remove the stems, reserving the stems for the stuffing.
2. Combine the lemon juice, sea salt, olive oil and lemon zest. Pour over the mushrooms.
3. Gently turn the mushrooms in the marinade. This is best done by hand.
4. After 30 minutes remove the mushrooms from the marinade and place stem-side up onto a non-stick dehydrator sheet, reserving the left over marinade for the stuffing.
5. Dehydrate the mushrooms for 1 hour at 52ºC (125ºF).
6. Reduce the heat to 46ºC (115ºF) and dehydrate for a further 4 hours.

Making the stuffing

1. Rinse and drain the walnuts.
2. Place the walnuts with the sesame seed into a food processor and process for a few seconds into a rough pulp.
3. Drain the sun-dried tomatoes and goji berries, reserving the liquid.
4. Add the mushroom stems, the mushroom marinade, tomatoes, goji berries, lemon juice and lemon zest to the food processor.
5. Process into a pâté adding some of the liquid from the tomatoes and goji berries if necessary.
6. Stir in the quinoa.
7. Add the parsley, sea salt and pepper to taste and mix well.
8. Remove the mushrooms from the dehydrator but leave them on the tray.
9. Divide the stuffing equally between the mushrooms, pressing it into the cavity and creating a small mound on each mushroom.
10. Return the mushrooms to the dehydrator and dehydrate for 2-6 hours at 46ºC (115ºF).

Continues on next page

For the Sour Cream

250ml (1 cup) cashew cream (p. 115)

1 tablespoon chopped parsley

1 tablespoon chopped chives

1 teaspoon apple cider vinegar

¼ teaspoon sea salt

freshly ground pepper

For the sour cream

1. Mix the cashew cream with the chopped parsley, chives, cider vinegar and sea salt.

To plate the mushrooms

1. Remove the mushrooms from the dehydrator and place each one onto a large dinner plate.
2. Serve with the sour cream by either generously pouring the cream over the mushrooms or serving the cream in a separate dish.
3. Grind fresh black pepper onto the sour cream.

> **TIP**
> Dehydration time very much depends on how soft you like your mushrooms. I like them soft and juicy. If you don't have a dehydrator, you can warm the mushrooms in the oven at the lowest temperature setting but reduce the time to one or two hours and check regularly.

NOTES

STUFFED TOMATOES WITH 'CHEESY' SAUCE

Tomatoes are best eaten in the summer, when they're not only available in abundance but also at their best – sweet and juicy.

Serves: 4
Equipment needed: food processor
Plan ahead: requires pre-soaking

INGREDIENTS

For the tomatoes

8 medium tomatoes (2 per person)

65g (½ cup) sun ower seeds, soaked for 8-12 hours

65g (1 packed cup) spinach, tough stems removed

1 carrot, chopped

4 sun-dried tomatoes, soaked for 2 hours

1 tablespoon apple cider vinegar

1 tablespoon extra virgin olive oil

4 teaspoons date & mulberry paste (p.105)

¼ teaspoon sea salt

50g (½ cup) pecan nuts, soaked for 8-12 hours

2 tablespoons sprouted buckwheat

8 basil leaves

For the 'cheesy' sauce

125ml (½ cup) cashew yoghurt or cream (p.116)

2 tablespoons nutritional yeast akes

1 teaspoon lemon juice

¼ teaspoon Herbamare or sea salt

1. Cut the tops off the tomatoes and scoop out the seeds to create cavities for stuffing.
2. Place the tomato tops with the sun ower seeds, spinach, carrot, drained sun-dried tomatoes, cider vinegar, olive oil, date and mulberry paste and sea salt into a food processor and process into a smooth pâté.
3. Rinse and drain the pecans, add them to the pâté and process again brie y, chopping the pecans roughly into the mix.
4. Stir the sprouted buckwheat into the mix.
5. Fill the cavities of the tomatoes with the stuffing and sit two tomatoes each onto dinner plates.
6. Mix the cashew yoghurt or cream with the nutritional yeast akes, lemon juice and salt.
7. Top each stuffed tomato with Cashew 'Cheese' Sauce and decorate it with basil leaves.

> **TIP**
> Any left over stuffing that doesn't fit into the tomatoes can be stored in a glass jar in the refrigerator for 2-3 days and used as a spread on crackers or lettuce leaves.

NOTES

FOOD HEROES
TOMATOES
SPINACH
BUCKWHEAT

MINI PEPPERS WITH NUT 'CHEESE'

Equipment needed: food processor, dehydrator (optional)
Plan ahead: requires dehydrating (optional)

INGREDIENTS

For the peppers

250g mini peppers

½ teaspoon sea salt

2 tablespoons extra virgin olive oil

For the nut 'cheese'

65g (½ cup) pine nuts

70g (½ cup) macadamia nuts

2 tablespoons lemon juice

1 tablespoon nutritional yeast akes

¼ teaspoon sea salt or herbamare

½ teaspoon garlic powder

A dash of cayenne pepper

1 spring onion, chopped finely

2 tablespoons chopped, fresh parsley

I create these mini peppers as an appetiser for parties but they also are great as a side dish with a large mixed salad.

1. Cut the peppers lengthwise in half.
2. Remove the seeds and ribs but keep the stem in place.
3. Rub with sea salt and olive oil and leave to marinate in the refrigerator overnight or dehydrate at 46°C (115°F) for 4-6 hours.
4. Place the pine nuts, macadamia nuts, lemon juice, yeast akes, salt, garlic powder and cayenne pepper into a food processor and pulse several times until you have a smooth nut paste.
5. Add the chopped spring onion and parsley and mix again.
6. Remove the peppers from the refrigerator or dehydrator and fill each pepper cavity with nut cheese.
7. Sprinkle with black pepper or paprika and serve.

> **TIP**
> Use the nut cheese to stuff other vegetables such as pieces of celery, carved out courgettes, button mushrooms or baby tomatoes for a colourful appetiser plate.

NOTES

FOOD HEROES

PEPPERS
ONION
HERBS

SPICY NORI BITES

Serves: makes 32 bite-sized squares
Equipment: dehydrator

INGREDIENTS

2 nori sheets

200ml (¾ cup) Thai green curry sauce (p.56)

8 cherry tomatoes, sliced

This is another lovely snack for an appetiser plate. It goes particularly well when arranged on a plate with the mini peppers (see page 54).

1. Fold each nori sheet 4 times to create the outlines for the squares.
2. Cut each sheet with scissors into 16 squares.
3. Lay the individual squares onto a dehydrator rack, shiny side down
4. Spread a small amount of curry sauce onto each square.
5. Place a slice of tomato into the middle of each nori sheet.
6. Dehydrate the bites for one hour on 52ºC (125ºF) and then at 46ºC (115ºC) for 12-24 hours until the bites are crisp.

> **TIP**
> These bites can be kept in an airtight container for a week. However, they may go a bit oppy, if there is any moisture left in the sauce. You can easily crisp them up by sticking them in the dehydrator for a few hours. Like all other dehydrated food you can make these in the oven!

NOTES

FOOD HEROES

NORI SEAWEED
TOMATOES
GINGER
HERBS

THAI GREEN CURRY KELP NOODLES

Kelp noodles are the fast food alternative to pasta. Rich in minerals, low in calories and filling, they are an ideal carrier for delicious sauces.

Serves: 4
Equipment needed: food processor
Plan ahead: requires pre-soaking

INGREDIENTS

For the noodles

1 pack kelp noodles

100g (½ cup) frozen peas, defrosted

100g (½ cup) frozen sweetcorn, defrosted

1 carrot, cut into match-sticks

1 pointed red pepper, sliced thinly

40g (1 cup) Hijiki seaweed or sea spaghetti, soaked for 15 minutes and drained

For the curry sauce

260g (2 cups) of cashews, soaked for 20 minutes

1 can (350ml) coconut water

2 tablespoons coconut oil

2 sticks lemon grass, outer leaves removed & chopped

4cm (1½") fresh ginger, chopped

3 cloves or garlic

1-3 green chilli, de-seeded

2 handfuls of fresh coriander or 3 tablespoons frozen

1 handful fresh basil or 1 tablespoon frozen

1 lime, zest and juice

4 tablespoons Tamari

1 teaspoon coconut sugar

1. Soak the kelp noodles in cold water while you prepare the sauce.
2. Rinse and drain the cashew nuts.
3. Place the cashew nuts with the coconut water, coconut oil, lemon grass, ginger, garlic, chillies, coriander, basil, lime zest & juice, Tamari and coconut sugar in a blender.
4. Blend at high speed for up to 2 minutes to create a smooth cream.
5. Rinse and drain the kelp noodles.
6. Cut the kelp noodles with scissors into a large bowl.
7. Add the peas, sweetcorn, carrot, red pepper and seaweed.
8. Add the curry sauce and mix all well by hand.
9. Leave to marinate for 15-30 minutes.

TIP

Like all good curries, this tastes even better the next day. Keep it in the refrigerator but remove it from the refrigerator at least half an hour before serving. You might even want to add 2-3 tablespoons of hot water to warm the dish slightly, which will bring out the avours better. Left over sauce can be used for kale chips, nori bites or frozen for another day's meal.

NOTES

FOOD HEROES
KELP
SEAWEED
HERBS

CARROT BURGERS

Serves: 4
Equipment: food processor, dehydrator
Plan ahead: requires dehydrating

INGREDIENTS

300g (2 cups) carrots, chopped

100g (1½ cups) celeriac, peeled & chopped

1 celery stick, chopped

70g (½ cup) macadamia nuts

65g (½ cup) sun ower seeds, ground into a our

40g (¼ cup) linseed, ground

2 tablespoon unpasteurised miso

¼-½ preserved lemon, chopped finely

2 teaspoons lemon juice

1 tablespoon chopped basil

1 tablespoon chopped parsley

No recipe book would be complete without a burger. This is my version and my little secret is the preserved lemon, which gives this burger a light flavour. Serve it with a big mixed salad, sour cream (page 52) and raw tomato ketchup (page 107).

1. Place the carrots, celeriac, celery and macadamia nuts into a food processor and pulse two or three times.
2. Add the ground sun ower seeds and linseed, miso, preserved lemon and lemon juice, and process into a pâté.
3. Add the chopped herbs and process again brie y to mix well.
4. Shape the dough into 8 burgers and place them on a non-stick dehydrator sheet.
5. Dehydrate for one hour at 52ºC (125ºF).
6. Flip the burgers onto a second dehydrator tray and remove the non-stick sheet.
7. Reduce the heat to 46ºC (115ºF) and dehydrate for a further 8-12 hours or until you reach the desired consistency.

TIP

If you don't have a dehydrator you can use an oven instead. Keep the temperature as low as your oven allows and keep the door slightly open. Alternatively you can serve the burgers un-dehydrated as a pâté.

NOTES

FOOD HEROES

ROOTS
CELERY
HERBS

Serves: 4
Equipment: spiraliser or vegetable peeler, blender
Plan ahead: requires pre-soaking

INGREDIENTS

2-3 medium courgettes

6 medium tomatoes, chopped

55g (¾ cup) sun-dried tomatoes, soaked for 2 hours

25g (¼ cup) goji berries, soaked for 2 hours

1 garlic clove

1 tablespoon dried mixed herbs

½ tablespoon smoked paprika

1 teaspoon onion powder

1 tablespoon extra virgin olive oil

50g (½ cup) walnuts, soaked overnight

2 tablespoons chopped fresh or frozen basil

Freshly ground black pepper to taste

COURGETTE RIBBONS WITH SMOKY TOMATO SAUCE

Every raw chef has their favourite tomato sauce. This is mine. This sauce is rich and satisfying and would also be delicious on parsnip & cauliflower rice (page 28).

1. Spiralise the courgettes into ribbons with a spiraliser.
2. Alternatively cut the courgettes into ribbons with a vegetable peeler.
3. Drain but don't rinse the sun-dried tomatoes and goji berries. Reserve the liquid of both.
4. Blend the tomatoes, sun-dried tomatoes, goji berries, garlic, mixed herbs, smoked paprika, onion powder and olive oil into a chunky sauce.
5. To adjust the avour add some of the sun-dried tomato liquid for more salty or the gojiberry liquid for more sweet.
6. Add the walnuts and basil and pulse brie y to break down the walnuts without grinding them down completely.
7. Season with pepper. Sundried tomatoes are usually very salty, so only add more salt if absolutely needed.
8. Divide the courgette ribbons between 4 plates, top with the tomato sauce and nut 'parmesan' (page 111).

> **TIP**
> In the summer, when tomatoes are in abundance and at their best, I like to make larger quantities of this sauce and freeze it in portions.

NOTES

FOOD HEROES
TOMATOES
WALNUTS
GARLIC

BEETROOT & COURGETTE ROULADE

A beautiful dish with courgette slices serving as the containers for the vegetables in a pink sauce. Any left over vegetables will be lovely the next day with a simple green salad.

Serves: 2 as a main or 4 as a starter
Equipment: mandolin (optional)

INGREDIENTS

For the vegetables

2 medium courgettes

1 large beetroot

1 small celeriac

2 tablespoons chopped parsley

1 tablespoon chopped basil

2 tablespoons black sesame seeds

1 litre water with 1 tablespoon sea salt for soaking

For the dressing:

3 tablespoons raw tahini

2 tablespoons cider vinegar

2 tablespoons hemp oil

1½ tablespoons Tamari

1 date

Freshly ground pepper

1. Slice one courgette lengthwise into thin slices approximately 2mm thick. This should make 6-8 slices.
2. Soak the courgette slices in salt water while you prepare the other vegetables.
3. Cut the second courgette, the beetroot and celeriac into short matchsticks by hand or on a mandolin and place them into a large bowl.
4. Blend or whisk the tahini, cider vinegar, hemp oil, Tamari, date and black pepper into a creamy dressing, adding a little water if the mix is too thick.
5. Pour the dressing over the vegetables and mix well by hand, 'massaging' the dressing into the vegetables. Leave the vegetables to marinate for 10-15 minutes.
6. Meanwhile remove the courgette slices from the salt water, rinse them and dry them with kitchen paper.
7. Shape each courgette slice into a ring and place them onto individual plates.
8. Add the chopped herbs to the vegetables and mix well.
9. Fill the courgette rings with the vegetables, squeezing some of the liquid out as you're lifting them out of the bowl.
10. Finally drizzle the remaining sauce around the courgette rings and sprinkle with black sesame seeds.

NOTES

FOOD HEROES

BEETROOT HERBS

Serves: 4-6
Equipment: mandolin or food processor (optional)

INGREDIENTS

1 red cabbage

2 teaspoons sea salt

2 tablespoons balsamic vinegar

½ tablespoon apple cider vinegar

2 teaspoons coconut nectar

1 teaspoon onion powder

¼ teaspoon ground cloves

35g (¼ cup) raisins, chopped

3 tablespoons extra virgin olive oil

freshly ground black pepper

SPICED RED CABBAGE

One of those raw dishes that has a surprisingly cooked appearance. I like to serve it with mushroom steaks, on its own in salad or for a festive dish with raw nut roast.

1. Slice the cabbage as thinly as you can, using a knife, a mandolin or a food processor.
2. Add 2 teaspoons of sea salt and massage the cabbage with your hands until it wilts and juices are being produced.
3. Leave the cabbage for 15-20 minutes while you prepare the dressing.
4. Mix the balsamic vinegar, cider vinegar, onion powder, ground cloves and coconut nectar into a smooth dressing.
5. Taste the cabbage. If it seems too salty, rinse with water before moving to the next step.
6. Next remove as much liquid from the cabbage as you can. Do this by taking a handful of cabbage out of the bowl and squeezing it between your hands to extract the liquid. Transfer the squeezed cabbage to a fresh bowl. Repeat this step until all cabbage has been drained.
7. Add the vinegar dressing, chopped raisins and olive oil to the cabbage and mix well.
8. Add freshly ground black pepper to taste.
9. Leave to marinate for at least 30 minutes. It tastes best if marinated overnight.

> **NOTE**
> Balsamic and red wine vinegar are not raw and can contain small amounts of lead. For this reason I normally use raw apple cider vinegar as this has real health benefits, including potassium and beneficial bacteria. However, in this recipe the balsamic vinegar adds a certain depth to the avour. In my opinion occasional use of balsamic or red wine vinegar in small amounts is safe.

NOTES

FOOD HEROES

CABBAGE

NUT 'ROAST'

Serves: 4-6
Equipment: food processor, dehydrator
Plan ahead: needs pre-soaking and dehydrating

INGREDIENTS

70g (½ cup) almonds, soaked for 8-12 hours

50g (½ cup) pecan nuts, soaked for 8-12 hours

65g (½ cup) sun ower seeds, soaked for 8-12 hours

7 sun-dried tomatoes, soaked for 2 hours

1 tablespoon goji berries, soaked for 2 hours

1 tomato, chopped

1 celery stick, chopped

2 teaspoons herbs de Provence

3 tablespoons extra virgin olive oil

¼-½ teaspoon sea salt

100g (1 cup) sliced mushrooms

1 tablespoon chopped parsley

I originally created this recipe for Christmas but I'm sure there are other occasions where this raw, not roasted at all, roast will be appreciated.

1. Rinse and drain the almonds, pecan nuts and sun ower seeds.
2. Drain the sun-dried tomatoes and goji berries, but retain the soaking water, in case you need a bit more liquid for the recipe.
3. Place the nuts, seeds, sun-dried tomato, goji berries, chopped tomato, chopped celery stick, dried herbs, olive oil and salt into the food processor and process roughly.
4. Add the mushrooms and process again to create a coarse pâté.
5. Place the pâté onto a non-stick dehydrator sheet and shape it into a rectangular loaf approximately 7cm thick.
6. Dehydrate for 1 hour at 52ºC (125ºF).
7. Reduce the heat to 46ºC (115ºF) and dehydrate for a further 4 hours.
8. Carefully turn the nut 'roast' loaf over and dehydrate for a further 6-8 hours to create the desired consistency. You want a crusty outer layer and a moist inside.
9. Cut into slices to serve with spiced red cabbage (page 61), raw cranberry relish (page 113) or apple sauce (page 73) and a large green salad.

> **TIP**
> Once it's dehydrated, slice it and freeze any left overs, which will make a great quick dinner when there's not enough time to make food. It also works well with the smoky tomato sauce (page 58).

NOTES

FOOD HEROES
NUTS
TOMATOES
MUSHROOMS

RAWSAGNE

Serves: 4-6
Equipment: mandolin, dehydrator (both optional)
Plan ahead: requires fermenting, pre-soaking and dehydrating

INGREDIENTS

For the cheese layer
1 portion macadamia nut cheese (p.117)

For the vegetable layers
2 medium courgettes
1litre water with 1 tablespoon sea salt
100g (2 cups) baby spinach
1 tablespoon extra virgin olive oil
100g (1 cup) mushrooms, sliced
2 tablespoons pitted Kalamata olives, sliced

Like a cooked lasagne, making a rawsagne is a bit time consuming, but it's well worth the effort. To make a delicious dish that can easily feed a large group of people, simply double the recipe and use a larger dish.

Preparing the courgette and spinach
1. Slice the courgettes lengthwise on a mandolin into thin slices.
2. Place the slices into a large bowl and cover with the salted water.
3. After 30 minutes remove the courgette slices and pat them dry with kitchen towel.
4. In a separate bowl place the spinach and olive oil and massage with your hands until the spinach starts to wilt.

For the tomato sauce (see ingredients list on next page)
1. Drain the sun-dried tomatoes and goji berries.
2. Rinse and drain the pecans.
3. Blend the tomatoes, sun-dried tomatoes, goji berries, garlic, basil, olive oil, onion powder, dried mixed herbs and sea salt into a smooth sauce.
4. Add the pecans and pulse once or twice to chop the pecans into the sauce. Alternatively chop the pecans by hand and stir them into the sauce.
5. Add freshly ground black pepper to taste.

Recipe continues on next page

TIP
The rawsagne does not have to be dehydrated, but it helps to intensify the avours and give it more of a cooked appearance. It's also lovely served warm straight from the dehydrator. Alternatively you can warm it gently in the oven.
Like any good lasagne, rawsagne tastes even better the next day. Any left-overs will keep in the refrigerator for 2-3 days or can be frozen.

FOOD HEROES
SPINACH
TOMATO
MUSHROOMS

For the tomato sauce

4 medium tomatoes, chopped

55g (¾ cup) sun-dried tomatoes, soaked for 2 hours

4 pitted dates, chopped

1 garlic clove

2 tablespoons chopped basil

1 tablespoon olive oil

1 teaspoon onion powder

1 teaspoon dried mixed herbs

¼ teaspoon sea salt

50g (½ cup) pecan nuts, soaked for 8-12 hours

freshly ground black pepper to taste

Layering the rawsagne

1. Use a 22cm (8.5") round or square baking dish.
2. Start by covering the base with a third of the courgette slices.
3. Add one third of the tomato sauce and spread it over the courgette.
4. Add half of the mushrooms and olives slices.
5. Spoon half of the macadamia cheese onto the dish. Use a teaspoon for this and place dollops of cheese next to each other with a little space in between.
6. Add half of the spinach to cover the cheese and press it down with your hands.
7. Repeat these steps one more time, starting with the courgette.
8. Finally top everything with the last third of the tomato sauce.
9. Place the dish into the dehydrator and dehydrate for 2-4 hours on 46ºC (115ºF).
10. Remove from the dehydrator and sprinkle with nut parmesan (page 111).
11. Serve on pre-warmed plates.

NOTES

CELEBRATE SWEET

*Life is uncertain,
eat dessert first.*

Ernestine Ulmer

I love sweet things. I'm also an avid campaigner for the reduction of sugars in our diet. I believe sugar has a lot to answer for – refined white sugar from sugar beets in particular. It not only contains zero nutrients but if overconsumed can create a toxic load on the liver. Yet in the raw food/health food world other sugars are sometimes used that are also not good for us if we consume too much. I see many raw food recipes brimming with agave syrup, honey or maple syrup, when in fact we need very little sweetener at all to create a tasty dessert.

My desserts, snacks and cake recipes are designed with low sugar in mind. Wherever possible I try to use a whole food like fruit or dried fruits to sweeten my dishes. My favourite sweetener being home-made date & mulberry paste (page 105). Another is coconut sugar crystals or coconut nectar. Agave has been pushed off its 'healthy' pedestal recently, since the discovery that it is very high in fructos. For me it still has a place in recipes that require a liquid, avour neutral sweetener, but please, use it sparingly. Xylitol, if made from birch bark, while highly processed, has no impact on blood sugar levels and therefore makes a good option for people with diabetes. Stevia is made from a plant and has very little effect on blood sugar levels. Personally I've never much liked the avour, so I don't use it. But do give it a try and if you like it, it's certainly an option. I also recommend you stay well away from any artificial sweeteners.

Be your own judge. If initially you find the recipe not sweet enough, then by all means, add a little more. However, keep in mind that sugar, like salt, is a avour our taste buds often numb to. By incrementally reducing the amount of sweetener we use, we help our taste buds recover and develop a sensitivity for more subtle, real avours. Once you've discovered this pleasure, anything swamped with sweetness will offend your senses. Your body will naturally make the choice towards less sweet and more nutrition. Feel free to substitute the sweetener in the following recipes with other alternatives.

If you've decided to eat for nutrition to help boost your immune system, then sweets should be treated as what they were always intended for – a treat. Cake every day is not a healthy choice, even if raw! Now go and enjoy these recipes.

Incan Chocolate Torte page 80

Serves: makes 12 slices

Equipment needed: food processor, blender, 22cm round pie tin with removable base

INGREDIENTS

For the crust

15g (¼ cup) unsweetened desiccated coconut

120g (1 cup) hazelnut or almond pulp left over from making nut milk

(alternatively use 1 cup ground almonds or hazelnuts)

60g (½ cup) sun ower seeds

75g (½ cup) dates

1 pinch sea salt

For the filling

3 ripe avocados

3 limes, juice and zest

60g (½ cup) coconut oil, melted

½-1 tablespoon vanilla extract

35g (¼ cup) coconut nectar

LIME PIE

Easy and quick to make, beautiful to look at and delicious to eat. An excellent recipe for raw cake beginners.

To make the crust

1. Sprinkle the coconut evenly onto the base of a 22cm pie tin.
2. Process all other ingredients in a food processor until they start to hold together but still retain some texture.
3. Press the dough into the base and up the sides of the pie tin.
4. Place the tin into the refrigerator while preparing the filling.

To make filling

1. Combine all ingredients for the filling and blend them until smooth.
2. Pour the mix into the base and refrigerate for 2-3 hours.
3. Remove the pie from the pie tin and decorate with lime zest or desiccated coconut.

> **TIP**
> If you don't use all of the pie straight away, you can freeze the remainder whole or in portions, providing the pie has not been left out of the refrigerator for more then one hour.

NOTES

FOOD HEROES

HAZELNUTS
AVOCADO
LIMES

ORANGE CACAO TORTE

Serves: makes 12 slices
Equipment needed: food processor, blender, 20cm or 22cm cake tin with removable base
Plan ahead: requires pre-soaking and freezing

INGREDIENTS

For the base

70g (½ cup) Brazil nuts, pre-soaked for 8-12 hours

50g (½ cup) pecan nuts, pre-soaked for 8-12 hours

70g (½ cup) sun ower seeds, ground

70g (½ cup) pitted dates

½ teaspoon vanilla powder

1 pinch sea salt

1 tablespoons cacao nibs

For the fruit layer

3 large oranges, peeled and filleted

For the cacao cream

65g (¾ cup) cacao powder

120g (½ cup) coconut oil, melted

70g (¼ cup) coconut nectar

1 teaspoon lemon juice

zest from one orange

1 tablespoon orange juice

1 teaspoon cinnamon

1 teaspoon allspice

1 pinch sea salt

3 ripe avocados

This is my favourite cacao cake recipe using avocados for the cacao cream.

To make the base

1. Rinse and drain the Brazil and pecan nuts. Chop the nuts roughly and put aside.
2. Combine the ground sun ower seeds, dates, vanilla powder and sea salt and process into a sticky dough.
3. Add the chopped nuts and cacao nibs and knead them into the dough.
4. Cover the base of the cake tin with cling film and then fit the cake rim onto the base.
5. Spread the dough onto the cling film covered cake tin base and press down firmly.
6. Place the cake tin in the freezer while you prepare the cacao cream.

To make the cacao cream

1. Blend the melted coconut oil, cacao powder, coconut nectar, lemon juice, orange juice and zest, cinnamon, allspice and sea salt into a smooth paste.
2. Add the avocado and blend again until the cream is completely smooth with no lumps.

To assemble the torte

1. Arrange the orange slices on the cake base to cover the whole base.
2. Spoon the cacao cream onto the oranges and spread out evenly.
3. Level the surface with a spatula.
4. Place the torte in its tin in the freezer for at least 4 hours.
5. Once the torte is frozen solid, remove it from the cake tin and transfer to a plate.
6. Leave the cake to defrost for one hour before slicing it into 12 pieces.
7. Decorate with cacao powder and orange zest.

Recipe continues on next page

FOOD HEROES

ORANGES
AVOCADO
NUTS & SEEDS

TIP

Freeze the torte whole or in portions. Any left-overs can be kept in the refrigerator for 3-4 days or placed back in the freezer, as long as it has not been left out of the refrigerator for more than one hour.

To fillet an orange, remove the peel including the white pith with a sharp knife. Then cut out the individual segments of the orange along their thin skin.

VARIATIONS

Try different fruit, such as raspberries, cherries or strawberries depending on the season.

NOTES

CACAO NIB OAT BARS

Serves: makes 12

Equipment needed: coffee grinder or blender to grind the sun ower seeds

INGREDIENTS

1 banana

2 teaspoons lemon juice

60g (½ cup) sun ower seeds, ground

60g (½ cup) raw rolled oats

70g (½ cup) Brazil nuts, chopped

65g (½ cup) cashew nuts, chopped

30g (¼ cup) raw cacao nibs

1 tablespoon maca powder (optional)

1 tablespoon coconut oil, melted

¼-½ teaspoon mixed spice (cinnamon, coriander, nutmeg, clove, pimento, ginger)

A truly low sugar snack sweetened with only one banana! Keep them at hand for when you don't have time for breakfast or as a travel snack that won't rock your blood sugar level.

1. Use a fork to mash up the banana with the lemon juice
2. Add all other ingredients and work into a sticky dough.
3. Spread the dough onto non-stick baking paper and shape it into a rectangle approximately 1.5cm (½") thick.
4. Score the dough with a knife into 12 bars.
5. Place the bars in the refrigerator to set for at least an hour.

TIPS AND VARIATIONS

Even faster would be to place everything into a food processor and blitz it into a dough. Try ground almonds instead of the sun ower seeds.

NOTES

FOOD HEROES

BANANA
LEMON
SUNFLOWER SEEDS

APPLE CRUMBLE

Serves: 4-6

Equipment needed: blender, food processor, dehydrator (optional)

Plan ahead: requires pre-soaking and dehydrating

INGREDIENTS

For the crumble

4 tablespoons raw rolled oats

2 tablespoons chia seeds

125ml (½) cup water

40g (¼ cup) pecan nuts, soaked for 8-12 hours

40g (¼ cup) almonds, soaked for 8-12 hours

40g (¼ cup) sun ower seeds, soaked for 8-12 hours

1 tablespoon lucuma or mesquite powder

1 tablespoon maca powder (optional)

1 teaspoon allspice

For the apple sauce

6 apples

6 dates

1 teaspoon cinnamon

60ml (¼ cup) water

40g (¼ cup) raisins, soaked for 1 hour

As soon as the leaves fall and the apples from the garden are so plentiful that we think we'll never manage to eat them all, I yearn for apple crumble. This is a raw, low sugar version.

For the crumble

1. Soak the oats and chia seeds in 125ml water for 20 minutes.
2. Rinse & drain the pecans, almonds and sun ower seeds.
3. Add the lucuma powder, maca powder, allspice and sea salt to the nuts and seeds and mix well.
4. Add the soaked oats and chia seeds with the soaking water and mix well.
5. Place on a non-stick dehydrator sheet in small clusters and dehydrate at no more than 46ºC/115ºF for 14 hours or until crisp.

For the apple sauce

1. Blend the apples with the dates, cinnamon and water to a smooth apple sauce.
2. Then stir the raisins into the sauce.
3. Place into a gratin dish and top with the crumble.
4. Dehydrate for 4-6 hours and serve warm with cashew yoghurt (page 116).

VARIATIONS

Instead of yoghurt you can serve it with cashew cream (page 115) or banana ice cream (page 75). This crumble is also delicious cold the next day for breakfast.
I always keep some form of buckwheat crunch in a jar, ready to use. So when I'm in a hurry I top the apple sauce with crunch to save me making the crumble.

NOTES

FOOD HEROES

APPLES
ALMONDS
CHIA SEEDS

BANANA ICE CREAM

The simplest ice cream in the world. It's so fast to make that I always have frozen banana in the freezer in case I suddenly need to produce a dessert.

Serves: 2-4
Equipment needed: blender
Plan ahead: requires frozen bananas

INGREDIENTS

3 bananas, frozen in individual bite-size pieces for at least 24 hours

2 teaspoons lemon juice

1 teaspoon vanilla powder

1. Place the frozen banana pieces into a high speed blender.
2. Add the lemon juice and vanilla powder.
3. Blend all at high speed into a uffy cream.
4. Serve immediately.

> **VARIATIONS**
> Gently fold in blueberries, goji berries or cacao nibs into the finished ice cream. Work fast so your ice cream doesn't melt prematurely.

> **TIP**
> Whenever you have bananas that look like they're just getting too ripe, chop them into bite-size chunks and freeze them. It's best to lay them out on a baking tray first and freeze them as individual pieces. Once frozen you can transfer them to a freezer bag or container. Freezing them as individual pieces has two benefits. Firstly your blender will be able to crunch the frozen pieces into a cream. Secondly you will be able to remove just the amount of banana you need and leave the rest frozen.

NOTES

**FOOD
HEROES**

**BANANAS
LEMON**

MACADAMIA LEMON BISCUITS

Serves: makes 20-30 biscuits

Equipment needed: food processor, dehydrator (optional), cookie cutter

INGREDIENTS

260g (2 cups) cashew nuts

140g (1 cup) macadamia nuts

120ml (½ cup) date & mulberry paste (p.105)

2 teaspoons lemon extract

3 tablespoons ground linseed

I love this simple recipe that reminds me a bit of shortbread. Of course these yummy biscuits are made without sugar, flour or butter. I use tiny heart shaped cookie cutters which make pretty, bite-sized biscuits.

1. Place the cashew nuts into a food processor and grind them into a our. Be careful not to over-process, at this point you don't want the nuts to release their oils.
2. Add the macadamia nuts, date & mulberry paste and lemon extract and process into a sticky but crunchy dough.
3. Add the ground linseed and mix well.
4. Spread the dough onto a non-stick dehydrator sheet approximately 1cm (0.4") thick.
5. Use a cookie cutter to cut individual shapes.
6. Dehydrate at no more than 46ºC (115ºF) for 12-18 hours or until dry.
7. Because of the high oil content in the macadamia nuts, the biscuits will still have a moist texture even after the long dehydration time. The oil will however set once you leave the cookies to cool.
8. Store in an airtight container in the refrigerator for up to a week.

VARIATIONS
Instead of dehydrating you can roll the dough into balls or small rolls and let them set in the refrigerator. They will be less dry and more chewy.

Like all dehydrator recipes you can also dry these cookies in the oven at a very low temperature.

NOTES

FOOD HEROES

NUTS
LEMON
LINSEED

APPLE & CRANBERRY OAT BAR

An excellent staple to have in the refrigerator for a quick snack at any time of the day. Great for kids lunch packs too.

Serves: makes 12 bars
Equipment needed: food processor, dehydrator
Plan ahead: requires pre-soaking and dehydrating

INGREDIENTS

130g (1 cup) cashew nuts, soaked for 20 minutes

70g (½ cup) pitted dates

35g (¼ cup) raw rolled oats

2 apples, peeled and cored

½ teaspoon allspice, mixed spice or cinnamon

100 (1 cup) pecan nuts, soaked for 8-12 hours

50g (¼ cup) fresh or frozen cranberries

3 tablespoons shelled hemp seed

1. Rinse and drain the cashew nuts.
2. Place the cashew nuts, dates, oats, apple pieces and allspice into a food processor and process until you have a smooth dough.
3. Add the pecans, cranberries and hemp seeds and process again to chop up the nuts and cranberries but leaving small pieces.
4. Spread the dough into a rectangle on a non-stick dehydrator sheet about 1 finger thick.
5. Score the dough into squares with a large knife and dehydrate at 46ºC (115ºF) for 6 hours.
6. Flip them onto a dehydrator tray and dehydrate a further 4-8 hours until you reach the desired consistency.

> **TIP**
> How long to dehydrate depends very much on the consistency you prefer. The longer you dehydrate the more 'cooked' the appearance and the more intense the avours. Try tasting a bit of bar at certain stages of the dehydration process to determine whether your bars need a little longer.

NOTES

FOOD HEROES
NUTS
APPLES
CRANBERRIES

TAHINI CACAO TRUFFLES

Serves: makes 20 balls
Equipment needed: food processor (optional)
Plan ahead: requires pre-soaking

INGREDIENTS

130g (½ cup) raw light tahini

35g (¼ cup) cacao butter, melted

1 tablespoon coconut oil

2 tablespoons coconut nectar

65g (¾ cup) raw cacao powder

1 tablespoon mesquite powder

½ tablespoon light hemp powder

1 teaspoon vanilla powder

12 Almonds (ideally soaked and dehydrated)

For rolling: cacao powder, sesame seeds, dried fruit powder, cinnamon, green tea matcha or desiccated coconut.

So quick and easy to make, apart from the rolling of the truffles which can be messy but so much fun, particularly the licking of fingers at the end. These truffles are a superfood heaven.

1. Mix the tahini, cacao butter, coconut butter, coconut nectar, cacao powder, maca powder, mesquite powder and vanilla powder in a food processor or by hand to make a sticky dough.
2. Divide the dough into 20 equal amounts. If the dough is too oily to handle, simply place it in the freezer for a few minutes to firm up.
3. One by one press an almond into each piece of dough and then roll it into a ball.
4. Roll each ball in a powder of your choice. It's nice to use different powders to create different truf e colours.
5. Place the balls in the refrigerator for 1-2 hours to firm them up.

VARIATION

Look for a light raw tahini, as some raw tahini can be quite bitter. Alternatively use any other type of nut butter, such as almond or cashew. Tahini is usually made from roasted sesame seeds and peanut butter is also not raw, but both would still make delicious truf es.

NOTES

FOOD HEROES
SEEDS
WALNUTS

INCAN CHOCOLATE TORTE

Serves: makes 12 or 16 slices
Equipment needed: food processor, blender, freezer, small saucepan, 22cm cake tin with removable base.
Plan ahead: needs pre-soaking and sprouting

INGREDIENTS

For the base

130g (1 cup) hazelnut pulp

120g (1 cup) cashew nuts

50g (½ cup) mulberries

For the cacao cake mix

110g (1 cup) walnuts, soaked overnight

200g (1½ cup) buckwheaties, ground (p.108)

85g (1 cup) raw cacao powder

70g (½ cup) coconut nectar

120ml (½ cup) water

2 teaspoons lemon juice

½-1 teaspoon vanilla powder

75g (½) Brazil nuts, soaked overnight & chopped

55g (½ cup) cacao nibs

For the golden berry jam

200g (1½ cup) golden berries (Incan berries)

100g (½ cup) dates, pitted

240ml (1 cup) water for soaking

1 tablespoon agar agar

60ml (¼ cup) water for the agar agar

For the cacao ganache

2 tablespoons raw cacao butter, melted

90g (¾ cup) coconut oil, melted

3 tablespoons coconut nectar

85g (1 cup) raw cacao powder

1 teaspoon cinnamon

This recipe was inspired by a traditional Viennese Sacher Torte with its indulgent layers of chocolate saturated sponge, apricot jam and chocolate icing. I decided to give it a tropical hint through the tart flavour of the Golden Berries (Physalis) and the touch of cinnamon in the chocolate ganache. It's an elaborate recipe, but well worth the effort!

To make the base

1. Combine the hazelnut pulp, cashew nuts and mulberries into a food processor and process into a smooth dough.
2. Cover the base of a 22cm cake tin with cling film and fit the cake tin ring.
3. Spread the dough out evenly to cover the whole base and press down firmly.
4. Freeze for 30-60 minutes.

To make the cacao cake mix

1. Rinse and drain the walnuts.
2. Place the walnuts with the buckwheaties flour, cacao powder, coconut nectar, water, lemon juice and vanilla powder into a food processor and blend into a smooth dough.
3. Rinse and drain the Brazil nuts and add with the cacao nibs to the dough.
4. Process the mix to break down the Brazil nuts and cacao nibs further, incorporating them into the dough.
5. Split the dough into two portions and use a rolling pin to roll one portion into a round layer, roughly the size of the cake tin.
6. Remove the cake from the freezer and lay the dough onto the base. Spread it out evenly with your fingers, covering any holes. Keep the other half of the dough in a covered bowl in the fridge.

To make the golden berry jam

1. Soak the golden berries and dates in 240ml water for 2 3 hours.
2. Drain the golden berries and dates, reserving the liquid.
3. Blend the fruit with 120ml (1/2 cup) of the soaking liquid until smooth. The seeds of the golden berries may still be visible. Just make sure it's no longer gritty.

Recipe continues on next page

4. Bring 60ml (1/4 cup) water to a slight boil in a small saucepan.
5. Add the agar agar powder and stir constantly until the agar is dissolved.
6. Add the agar agar liquid to the berries and blend into a smooth jam.
7. Remove the cake from the freezer and spread half of the jam onto the cacao cake mix, then return the cake to the freezer for 30 minutes.

To add the next two layers

1. Remove the torte from the freezer and add the remainder of the cacao cake mix as a next layer.
2. Spread out evenly.
3. Add the remainder of the jam and spread out evenly.
4. Place the torte back into the freezer for at least 4 hours or overnight.
5. Remove the torte from the freezer.
6. Carefully remove the torte from the cake tin and place it on a large plate.
7. Leave the cake to defrost for 1 hour.

To make the cacao ganache

1. Combine the melted cacao butter, melted coconut oil, coconut nectar, cacao powder and cinnamon in a blender.
2. Blend until smooth.
3. Ensure the top of the torte has reached room temperature. Too cold a surface will make your ganache go hard too quickly.
3. Pour the mix over the top of the cake and spread it evenly with a spatula, also covering the sides of the cake.
4. Work quickly as the ganache will set fairly fast.
5. Decorate by drizzling ganache on top in an organised or random pattern – be creative!

NOTES

TIP

Use a warm, serrated knife to gently cut through the harder cacao ganache, then slice through the rest of the cake. The cake will store well in the refrigerator for three days or you can freeze the individual slices for later use.

FOOD HEROES

HAZELNUTS
BUCKWHEAT
BERRIES

RAW ROCKY ROAD

Thick, crunchy chocolate slices. A fabulous treat that also makes a lovely gift for a good friend who's in need of a bit of chocolate love.

Serves: makes 12-16 slices
Equipment needed: food processor

INGREDIENTS

80g (1 cup) desiccated coconut

100g (¾ cup) macadamia nuts

80g (½ cup) raw cacao butter, melted

85g (1 cup) raw cacao powder

3 tablespoons coconut sugar

1 tablespoon coconut oil, melted

1 tablespoon maca powder

2 teaspoon vanilla powder

1 pinch sea salt

100g (1 cup) Cinnamon Buckwheat Crunch (p.15)

1. Place the coconut and macadamia nuts into the food processor and process until the nuts are broken down and are starting to release their oils.
2. Add the cacao butter, cacao powder, coconut sugar, coconut butter, maca powder, vanilla powder and salt to the nuts and process into a runny dough.
3. Pour the chocolate/nut mix into a bowl and stir in the buckwheat crunch by hand.
4. Pour the dough onto a large dinner plate, spreading out the dough onto the plate not covering the rim.
5. Place a second dinner plate up-side-down on top as a lid and keep it in the refrigerator for 2 hours to set.
6. Remove the rocky road from the refrigerator and carefully slice into 12 wedges.

> **VARIATION**
> Instead of the cinnamon buckwheat crunch you can also use chopped almonds, walnuts, sun ower seeds, pumpkin seeds, raisins or goji berries. Experiment and create your own unique avour.

NOTES

FOOD HEROES
NUTS
SEEDS

BLACK FOREST CHERRY TUMBLER

Serves: 4-6
Equipment needed: blender, 4 to 6 glass tumblers or wine glasses for serving

INGREDIENTS

For the cream

½ recipe cashew cream (p.115)

1 tablespoon coconut nectar

1 teaspoon vanilla powder

For the crunch

100g (1 cup) Cinnamon Buckwheat Crunch (p.15)

For the cacao mousse

2 tablespoons raw cacao butter, melted

8 tablespoons raw cacao powder

1 tablespoon maca powder

1 teaspoon vanilla powder

2 tablespoons coconut nectar

2 avocados

For the fruit layer

200g (2 cups) fresh or frozen pitted cherries

All my favourite sweet things combined into one luxurious dish. This is one for special occasions.

For the cream

1. Mix the cashew cream with the coconut nectar and vanilla powder using a whisk.
2. Beat the cream with the whisk to introduce some air and make the cream more uffy.
3. Set aside.

For the cacao mousse

1. Place the cacao butter, cacao powder, maca powder, vanilla powder and coconut nectar into the blender and blend into a smooth paste.
2. Cut the avocados in half, remove the stone and scoop the esh out of the skins into the blender.
3. Blend the avocados into the cacao paste until you have a smooth mousse.

Assembling the tumblers

1. Place an equal amount of Cinnamon Buckwheat Crunch into each glass.
2. Divide the cherries between the glasses.
3. Divide the cacao mousse between the glasses.
4. Top with the cashew cream.

> **VARIATION**
> You can also just use chopped nuts and seeds instead of the Buckwheat Crunch. Try different fruit, such as raspberries or strawberries.

FOOD HEROES
CHERRIES
AVOCADOS
BUCKWHEAT

NOTES

GOOSEBERRY CHIA MOUSSE

Serves: 4
Equipment needed: blender

INGREDIENTS

260g (2 cups) cashew nuts, soaked for 30 minutes

240ml (1 cup) water

1 punnet fresh gooseberries, stems removed

½ lemon, juiced

1 tablespoon baobab powder

1 teaspoon vanilla essence

60ml (¼ cup) coconut nectar

85g (½ cup) chia seed

A refreshing, light dessert which also makes a delicious breakfast pudding.

1. Reserve a few nice looking gooseberries for decorating.
2. Blend all ingredients except the chia seeds in a blender at high speed until you achieve a smooth cream.
3. Add the chia seed and blend brie y to mix well.
4. Place the mousse in the fridge for two or three hours to set.

VARIATION
Try other berries such as raspberries or strawberries. Or create two different coloured mousses and layer them in glass jars for a colourful presentation.

NOTES

FOOD HEROES
CHIA SEEDS
LEMON

Lemon Mango 'Cheese' Cake page 86

LEMON MANGO 'CHEESE' CAKE

If there is one dish that can turn people onto raw food, it's probably raw 'cheese' cake. I love this particular combination of the sweetness of the mango and the tartness of the lemon cheese mix. But do try other fruit. Re-freeze any left over cake for a rainy day.

Serves: makes 12-16 slices
Equipment needed: food processor, blender, 20cm or 22cm cake tin with removable base
Plan ahead: pre-soaking and freezing.

INGREDIENTS

For the 'cheese' filling

390g (3 cups) cashew nuts, soaked for 30 minutes

4 Lemons, zest and juice

120ml (½ cup) coconut nectar

180ml (¾ cup) coconut oil, melted

1 tablespoon baobab powder

1 teaspoon vanilla powder

Up to a ½ cup of water to facilitate blending

For the crust

130g (1 cup) sun ower seeds

70g (½ cup) dates

50g (½ cup) pecan nuts

1 pinch of sea salt

2 tablespoons desiccated coconut

For the topping

3 ripe mangos, peeled and stone removed

1-2 dates, only if the mango isn't sweet enough

For the cheese filing

1. Add all ingredients for the cheese filling into a blender, except the water.
2. Blend on high speed into a smooth cream, adding water little by little to facilitate blending. You're aiming for a thick double cream consistency.

For the crust

1. Place the sun ower seeds, dates and sea salt into a food processor and process into a sticky dough.
2. Add the pecan nuts and chop them roughly into the dough.
3. Sprinkle the desiccated coconut evenly onto the base of a round cake tin.
4. Spread the dough onto the base, being careful to not disturb the coconut too much and press down firmly.

Assembling the cake

1. Add the cheese cake mix onto the crust and spread out evenly.
2. Place in the freezer for 3-4 hours.
3. Blend the mangos and lemon juice until completely smooth. You may have to strain them through a sieve if they are too stringy.
4. Pour the mango puree onto the frozen cheese cake and return to the freezer.
5. Freeze for 24 hours.
6. Remove from the freezer.
7. Gently remove the cake from the tin and transfer to a plate.
8. Leave the cake to defrost for an hour (or less in hot weather) and carefully slice into 12 wedges.

FOOD HEROES
MANGO
LEMONS
NUTS & SEEDS

Recipe variations on next page

VARIATIONS
Try different fruit purées, such as raspberries, blackberries or strawberries. Decorate with grated chocolate. Split the cheese and fruit into half and create 4 layers instead of just two. Let your imagination run free.

NOTES

How can a nation be called great if its bread tastes like Kleenex.

Julia Child

BREADS, CRACKERS & WRAPS

Breads and crackers complete the raw food kitchen by adding foods that allow us to wrap and envelope the various raw vegetable goodies. Bread is perhaps one of the hardest foods for people to do without. We're so used to making a quick sandwich and they're also the food that is most available to buy ready made when on the go.

Raw breads and crackers are different, but they fill the gap well. As you start to eat more raw, fresh foods, the yearning for bread lessens, but occasionally it's nice to have something you can dip into the guacamole, lather with nut cheese or wrap around some freshly cut vegetables.

So here are a few of my favourite breads, wraps and crackers. The Carrot & Onion Bread in this section has been enjoyed by everybody I've served it to, whether they are into raw food or not. And let me assure you, it absolutely does not taste of Kleenex.

MOROCCAN SEED CRACKERS

Easy to make, these are great crackers for beginners. Lovely with a dip or broken into smaller pieces over a salad.

Serves: makes 2 trays
Equipment needed: blender, dehydrator
Plan ahead: requires pre-soaking and dehydrating

INGREDIENTS

2 garlic cloves

160g (1 cup) linseed (flax seed)

85g (½ cup) chia seeds

70g (½ cup) pumpkin seeds

65g (½ cup) sunflower seeds

65g (¼ cup) black or white sesame seeds

1 tablespoon nori flakes

950ml (4 cups) of water

1 tablespoon Tamari

1 teaspoon ground cumin

1 teaspoon ground coriander

1 teaspoon ground ginger

1. Blend the garlic with 240ml (1 cup) of the water until the garlic is completely broken down. If you have a powerful blender you don't even need to peel the garlic, as there is goodness in the dry skin.
2. In a large bowl combine the linseeds, chia seeds, pumpkin seeds, sunflower seeds and sesame seeds.
3. Add the garlic water, remaining plain water, nori flakes, Tamari, ground cumin, coriander and ginger to the seeds and mix well.
4. Leave the mix to soak for 4 hours.
5. Stir occasionally to distribute the chia seeds evenly – they have a tendency to clump.
6. Spread the seed mix onto non-stick dehydrator sheets and dehydrate for 4-6 hours.
7. Carefully flip the sheets onto dehydrator mesh trays and remove the non-stick sheet.
8. Dehydrate the crackers for another 6-8 hours or until crisp.
9. Break the dried seed sheets into random crackers.

> **TIP**
> If you don't have a dehydrator, use your oven on the lowest setting (50°C max) with the door slightly open. The crackers can be stored in an airtight container for 2 weeks.

NOTES

FOOD HEROES
GARLIC
NORI
CHIA

ITALIAN SEED CRACKERS

A variation on the Moroccan seed crackers, these are Italian style with tomatoes and Mediterranean herbs, and just as easy to make.

Serves: makes 2 trays
Equipment needed: blender, dehydrator
Plan ahead: requires pre-soaking and dehydrating

INGREDIENTS

2 garlic cloves
4 plum tomatoes, chopped
80g (½ cup) linseed (flax seed)
80g (½ cup) linseed, ground
85g (½ cup) chia seeds
65g (½ cup) sunflower seeds
65g (¼ cup) white sesame seeds
950ml (4 cups) of water
1 teaspoon dried basil
1 teaspoon dried oregano
½ teaspoon sea salt or herbamare
A few turns of the pepper mill

1. Blend the garlic and tomatoes with 240ml (1 cup) of the water until completely broken down. If you have a powerful blender you don't even need to peel the garlic, as there is goodness in the dry skin.
2. In a large bowl combine the linseeds, ground linseeds, chia seeds, sunflower seeds and sesame seeds.
3. Add the tomato water, remaining plain water, dried basil, dried oregano, sea salt and black pepper. Leave the mix to soak for 4 hours.
4. Stir occasionally to distribute the chia seeds evenly – they have a tendency to clump up.
5. Spread the seed mix onto non-stick dehydrator sheets and dehydrate for 4-6 hours.
6. Carefully flip the sheets onto dehydrator mesh trays and remove the non-stick sheet.
7. Dehydrate the crackers for another 6-8 hours or until crisp.
8. Break the dried seed sheets into random crackers.

> **TIP**
> If you don't have a dehydrator, use your oven on the lowest setting (50°C max) with the door slightly open. The crackers can be stored in an airtight container for 2 weeks.

NOTES

FOOD HEROES

GARLIC
TOMATO
SEEDS

BEETROOT & ROSEMARY CRACKERS

Serves: makes 36 crackers
Equipment needed: food processor, dehydrator
Plan ahead: requires pre-soaking and dehydration

INGREDIENTS

130g (1 cup) sunflower seeds, soaked 8-12 hours

1 medium beetroot, scrubbed and chopped

1 small red onion, peeled and chopped

125ml (½ cup) water

½ lemon, juiced

¼ teaspoon sea salt

1 tablespoon finely chopped, fresh rosemary

80g (½ cup) linseed, ground

This is the first cracker recipe I ever created and it's still one of my favourites. Don't be temped to overdo it on the rosemary, it's a very powerful taste and you want to keep it subtle.

1. Place the sunflower seeds, beetroot, onion, water, lemon juice and sea salt into a food processor and process into a pulp.
2. Add the rosemary and linseed and mix well.
3. Add some more water if necessary. You want a thick dough that's still easy to spread.
4. With a spatula or palette knife spread the dough thinly onto a non-stick dehydrator sheet. It will cover a 40cm x 40cm square.
5. Score the dough into equal squares by pressing a knife into it.
6. Dehydrate for 8 hours at no more than 46°C (115°F).
7. Flip the crackers onto a dehydrator tray and remove the non-stick sheet.
8. Dehydrate for a further 8 hours or until the crackers are crisp.
9. Remove from the dehydrator and leave to cool. Store in an airtight box.

> **TIP**
> Crackers usually store well in an airtight container. They don't need to go into the refrigerator, as long as they are completely dry when stored. They may lose their crunch after a week or so, but you can just crisp them up again by returning them to the dehydrator for a few hours.

NOTES

FOOD HEROES
BEETROOT
ONION
HERBS

YELLOW PEPPER & SAFFRON CRACKERS

Serves: makes 36 crackers
Equipment needed: blender, food processor, dehydrator
Plan ahead: requires pre-soaking and dehydrating

INGREDIENTS

2 yellow peppers, de-seeded and chopped

2 pinches saffron

125ml (½ cup) water

130g (1 cup) sunflower seeds, soaked for 8-12 hours

½ lime, juiced

¼ teaspoon sea salt

80g (½ cup) golden linseed, ground

1 tablespoon black sesame seeds

I created this recipe on one of my retreats in Portugal when I wanted to have a delicate cracker with a bright yellow colour. These are stunning looking crackers that go particularly well with a green guacamole.

1. Blend the yellow pepper with the saffron and water until completely broken down.
2. Rinse and drain the sunflowers and place them into a food processor with the yellow pepper mix, lime juice and sea salt.
3. Process into a smooth pulp.
4. Add the linseed and black sesame seeds and mix well.
5. Remove the mix from the food processor and stir in the sesame seeds by hand.
6. With a spatula or palette knife spread the dough thinly onto a non-stick dehydrator sheet. It will cover a 40cm x 40cm square.
7. Score the dough into equal squares by pressing a knife into it.
8. Dehydrate for 8 hours at no more than 46ºC (115ºF).
9. Flip the crackers onto a dehydrator tray and remove the non-stick sheet.
10. Dehydrate for a further 8 hours or until the crackers are crisp.
11. Remove from the dehydrator and leave to cool. Store in an airtight box.

VARIATIONS

Use red or orange peppers to create different coloured crackers.
Replace the saffron with ground turmeric. Turmeric, like saffron gives a beautiful deep yellow colour.

NOTES

FOOD HEROES

PEPPERS
SEEDS

GARLIC CROUTONS

Delicious and crunchy on soups or salads.

Equipment needed: food processor, dehydrator
Plan ahead: requires pre-soaking and dehydrating

INGREDIENTS

130g (1 cup) hazelnut pulp (or ground hazelnuts)

140g (1 cup) psyllium husk

80g (½ cup) linseeds (flax seeds), ground

3 garlic cloves, peeled

2 tablespoons nutritional yeast flakes

1 tablespoon extra virgin olive oil

1 teaspoon dried mixed Italian herbs

½ teaspoon sea salt

125ml (½ cup) water

1. Mix all ingredients in a large bowl by hand until you get a soft sticky dough. Alternatively process in a food processor.
2. Place the dough onto a non-stick dehydrator sheet and with a rolling pin roll the dough into a square to approximately 1.5cm (½") thickness.
3. Score the dough into small cubes.
4. Dehydrate at 46°C (115°F) for 4-6 hours.
5. Flip the dough onto a dehydrator mesh tray, remove the non-stick sheet and dehydrate for a further 10-12 hours or until completely dry and crispy.
6. The croutons will store in an airtight container for up to 3 weeks.

> **TIP**
> Instead of croutons, score the dough into soldiers before dehydrating and use with dips.

NOTES

FOOD HEROES

NUTS
GARLIC
HERBS

CARROT & ONION BREAD

Serves: makes 12 slices of bread
Equipment needed: blender, food processor, dehydrator
Plan ahead: requires pre-soaking and dehydrating

INGREDIENTS

160g (1 cup) sprouted buckwheat

150g carrot, chopped

2 shallots, peeled and halved

240ml (1 cup) water

60ml (¼ cup) Tamari

4 teaspoons date & mulberry paste (p.105)

1 teaspoon sea salt

130g (1 cup) sunflower seeds, ground

70g (1 cup) psyllium husk

40g (¼ cup) linseed, ground

3 tablespoons chia seed

2-3 tablespoons sesame seeds

Just like real bread. Top it with avocado and tomato, or try it with coconut butter, caramalised onions (page 104) and sprinkle of sea salt.

1. Place the sprouted buckwheat, chopped carrot, shallots, Tamari, water, date & mulberry paste and salt into the food processor and blend into a purée.
2. Add the ground sunflower seeds, phsyllium husk, ground linseed and chia seed to the food processor into a dough.
3. Add a little more water if necessary, you want the consistency of a moist bread dough that sticks well together.
4. Shape the dough into a loaf approximately 17cm (7") long and roll it in the sesame seed to create the 'crust'.
5. Place the loaf onto a non-stick dehydrator sheet.
6. With a sharp knife, score the top of the bread to mark 12 slices.
7. Dehydrate for 3 hours at 52ºC (125ºF), then reduce the temperature and dehydrate for 12 hours at 46ºC (115ºF).
8. Remove the bread from the dehydrator and slice according to the scoring.
9. Lay the individual slices onto a dehydrator tray and dehydrate for a further 3-4 hours at 46ºC (115ºF). Turn the slices over half way through the drying process.

TIP
If you don't have a dehydrator, use your oven on the lowest setting (50ºC max) with the door slightly open. The bread slices can be stored in an airtight container in the refrigerator for 3-4 days or frozen.

NOTES

FOOD HEROES
CARROTS
ONIONS
CHIA SEEDS

CHIA SEED PIZZA CRUST

Serves: makes 10-12 small pizza rounds
Equipment needed: food processor, dehydrator
Plan ahead: requires pre-soaking and dehydrating

INGREDIENTS

1 shallot, peeled & quartered

1 garlic, peeled

1 small courgette (zucchini), chopped

1 tablespoon nori flakes

½ teaspoon sea salt

60ml (¼ cup) water

2 tablespoons chopped fresh parsley

65g (½ cup) sunflower seeds, soaked 8-12 hours

70g (½ cup) pumpkin seeds, soaked 8-12 hours

65g (½ cup) sesame seeds, soaked 8-12 hours

140g (1 cup) buckwheaties (p.108)

2 tablespoons chia seeds, soaked in 240ml (1 cup) water for 8-12 hours.

3 tablespoons linseeds (flax seeds) ground into a flour

I always try to have a few pizza crusts in my store cupboard for a quick meal. Top with any combination of nut cheese (page 117), raw ketchup (page 107), marinated mushrooms (page 106), caramelised onions (page 104) and fresh greens and vegetables.

1. Place the shallot, garlic, courgette, nori flakes, sea salt and water into the food processor and process into a pulp.
2. Add the parsley and pulse 2 or 3 times to mix well.
3. Rinse and drain the sunflower seeds, pumpkin seeds and sesame seeds and add them to the food processor, along with the dried buckwheat.
4. Process into a rough dough.
5. Add the soaked chia seeds with the soaking water and ground linseeds to the dough and mix well.
6. Place approximately 2 tablespoons of dough into one quarter of a non-stick dehydrator sheet and spread it out into a circle approximately 20cm (8") in diameter. Place 4 rounds onto one dehydrator sheet.
7. Dehydrate at 52ºC (125ºF) for one hour, then reduce the temperature to 46ºC (115ºF) and dehydrate for a further 8 hours.
8. Flip the pizza bases onto a dehydrator mesh tray and dehydrate for a further 8-10 hours or until completely dry and crisp.

VARIATIONS
Adding a teaspoon of Spirulina adds a great flavour too. An excellent way to get these important mineral rich superfoods into a meal.

NOTES

FOOD HEROES
ONION
SEAWEED
SEEDS

GREEN CORN WRAPS

Stuff them with left over vegetables, leafy greens, chopped carrots, avocado, cashew sour cream, sprouts or whatever your heart desires

Equipment needed: blender, dehydrator
Plan ahead: requires pre-soaking and dehydrating

INGREDIENTS

1 courgette, chopped

200g (2 cups) corn, fresh or from frozen

100g (1 cup) baby spinach

1 garlic clove

¼ teaspoon sea salt

1 teaspoon ground coriander

¼ teaspoon cayenne pepper

125ml (½ cup) water

80g (½ cup) linseed, ground

3 tablespoons extra virgin olive oil

1. Blend the courgette, corn, baby spinach, garlic, sea salt, ground coriander, cayenne pepper and water into a smooth puree.
2. Add the ground linseed and nutritional yeast flakes and blend again until creamy.
3. Add more water if necessary. You want to achieve a pancake type batter.
4. Pour the batter in portions onto non-stick dehydrator sheets and spread them out in circles as thin as you can.
5. Dehydrate at 42ºC (105ºF) for 3-4 hours.
6. Flip the wraps onto dehydrator trays and dry for a further 2-3 hours.
7. Store in sealed plastic bags or containers in the refrigerator for 2-3 weeks.

TIP
Leave out the olive oil. Score the batter into triangles before dehydrating and dehydrate until completely crisp for green corn chips.

NOTES

FOOD HEROES

LINSEED
SPINACH
GARLIC

WALNUT & RAISIN BREAD

Equipment needed: food processor, dehydrator
Plan ahead: requires pre-soaking and dehydrating

INGREDIENTS

160g (1 cup) sprouted buckwheat

1 banana, chopped

1 apple, cored and chopped

240ml (1 cup) water

60g (½ cup) sunflower seeds, pre-soaked for 8-12 hours

60g (½ cup) pumpkin seeds, pre-soaked for 8-12 hours

70g (1 cup) psyllium husk

50g (½ cup) walnuts, pre-soaked for 8-12 hours and chopped

40g (¼ cup) linseed, ground

30g (¼ cup) raisins, chopped

3 tablespoons chia seed

1 teaspoon allspice or mixed spice

1 teaspoon cinnamon

Nothing beats a slice of this comforting bread, straight from the dehydrator with a little coconut butter and a cup of tea.

1. Place the sprouted buckwheat, banana, apple and water into the food processor and blend into a purée.
2. Rinse and drain the sunflower and pumpkin seeds, add them to the food processor and chop them into the purée.
3. Transfer the mix into a large bowl, add the psyllium husk, walnuts, linseed, raisins, chia seeds and spices and knead it into a strong dough.
4. Add a little more water if necessary, you want the consistency of a moist bread dough that sticks well together.
5. Shape the dough into a loaf approximately 17cm (7") long.
6. Place the loaf onto a non-stick dehydrator sheet.
7. With a sharp knife, score the top of the bread to mark 12 slices.
8. Dehydrate for 3 hours at 52°C (125°F), then reduce the temperature and dehydrate for 12 hours at 46°C (115°F).
9. Remove the bread from the dehydrator and slice according to the scoring.
10. Lay the individual slices onto a dehydrator tray and dehydrate for a further 6 hours at 46°C (115°F).

VARIATION

To create a sweeter loaf, use 2 bananas and leave out the apple. Try different dried fruit instead of raisins, such as mulberries, goji berries or unsweetened cranberries.

NOTES

FOOD HEROES

SEEDS
WALNUTS
BANANA

BASICS

*Sometimes it's
the basic things
that make life
truly special.*

Gabriela Lerner

I always have basics in the store cupboard and in my refrigerator. Basics are those simple foods that need a little preparation but can lift a recipe up to greater heights. They are either dehydrated so they store well in glass jars, or they can be kept in the refrigerator for a few days or frozen.

Many of my recipes will refer to this section and if you really want to eat raw on a daily basis, then it's best to always have some of these basic items ready to use. Think of them as replacements to the usual mayonnaise, ketchup, chutneys and pickles that you may have in your cupboard.

Nut 'Parmesan' page 111

Equipment needed: dehydrator

INGREDIENTS

2 large sweet onions, thinly sliced

60ml (¼ cup) Tamari or unpasteurised miso

1½ tablespoons sweetener of your choice, such as date & mulberry paste (p.105), coconut nectar, coconut sugar, agave syrup

CARAMELISED ONIONS

Caramelised onions are a staple to keep in the refrigerator and add to salads, noodle dishes, food wraps and soups. Choose large, sweet onions that don't have a strong onion flavour!

1. Place the onion, Tamari, date paste and olive oil in a large bowl.
2. Mix well and leave to marinate for 30 minutes.
3. Drain the onions and reserve the liquid.
4. Spread onto non-stick dehydrator sheets and dehydrate for 1 hour at 52ºC (125ºF).
5. After one hour reduce the temperature to 46ºC (115ºF) and dehydrate for a further 8-16 hours.
6. You can dehydrate them until they are completely crisp or just slightly on the chewy side.
7. Remove the onions from the dehydrator sheets and store them in an airtight jar in the refrigerator for up to 3 weeks depending on how dry they were dehydrated.

TIP

If you don't have a dehydrator you can also make these onions in the oven. Keep the temperature at 50ºC or lower, with the door slightly open.

Very strong onions can be soaked in salty water for an hour, then rinse, drain and dry them with kitchen paper before marinating them. Use the marinade as a flavour in savoury recipes, such as Carrot & Onion bread (page 97).

NOTES

FOOD HEROES

ONIONS

DATE & MULBERRY PASTE

Serves: makes approximately 500ml
Equipment needed: blender, dehydrator
Plan ahead: requires pre-soaking

INGREDIENTS

140g (1 cup) dates, pitted

100g (1 cup) mulberries

480ml (2 cups) water

In my opinion it's always best to sweeten your dishes with whole foods. When you use whole foods you not only get the sugars but also all the vitamins, minerals and fibre. This easy to make paste is great for use in dressings, snacks, cakes and smoothies.

1. Soak the dates and mulberries in the water for at least 4 hours or overnight.
2. Blend the dates and mulberries in the soaking water until completely smooth.
3. Store in a glass jar in the refrigerator or pour the paste into ice cub trays and freeze them.
4. Once frozen, remove the cubes from the trays and store them in a freezer bag or container in the freezer. One cube is approximately 2 teaspoons of sweetener.
5. Defrost the cubes before using in recipes.

VARIATIONS
If you don't have mulberries, you can use only dates (2 cups in that case) but the paste will be a lot sweeter. Try also a mix of date and goji berries or single fruit such as dried apricot or fig.

NOTES

FOOD HEROES

DATES
MULBERRIES

MARINATED MUSHROOMS

A must-have staple to keep in the refrigerator. Sprinkle them onto salads, soups, pizza or stuff them into vegetable wraps.

Equipment needed: dehydrator

INGREDIENTS

250g (2 cups) mushrooms (white, brown, shitake or oyster)

Marinade 1

3 tablespoons Tamari

3 tablespoons olive oil

Marinade 2

½ lemon, juiced

3 tablespoons extra virgin olive oil

2 pinches sea salt

1 tablespoon chopped parsley

1. Clean the mushrooms and remove the stems if necessary.
2. Slice the mushrooms thinly, approximately the thickness of a £1 coin.
3. Mix the ingredients for either marinade 1 or 2 and pour it over the mushrooms.
4. Leave the mushrooms to marinate for 10-15 minutes.
5. Spread the mushrooms onto non-stick dehydrator sheets and dehydrate for 1 hour at 52ºC (125ºF).
6. After one hour reduce the heat to 46ºC (115ºF) and dehydrate for a further 8-12 hours until the mushrooms are dry and chewy.

VARIATION

Sprinkle the mushrooms with shelled hemp seeds (hemp hearts) or sesame seeds before dehydrating. Add garlic, onion or chilli to the dressing for an extra kick.

NOTES

FOOD HEROES
MUSHROOMS

RAW TOMATO CHUTNEY

Serves: 300g
Equipment needed: blender, dehydrator (optional)
Plan ahead: requires pre-soaking and dehydrating

INGREDIENTS

6 sun-dried tomatoes, soaked for 2 hours

1 tablespoon dried golden berries, soaked for 2 hours

250g tomatoes, chopped

1-2 dates (depending on sweetness of tomatoes)

1 tablespoon lemon juice (optional depending on sweetness of tomatoes)

½ teaspoon garlic powder

1 teaspoon paprika

1 teaspoon curry powder

½ teaspoon sea salt

1 tablespoon chia seeds

The first things that had to go from our refrigerator when we started clean, unprocessed eating, were the bottles of ketchup and jars of mayonnaise. This raw tomato chutney is a wonderful replacement for ketchup, you won't miss the bottled stuff at all.

1. Rinse and drain the soaked sun-dried tomatoes.
2. Drain the golden berries but reserve the liquid.
3. Blend the chopped tomatoes with the sun-dried tomatoes, golden berries, dates, garlic powder, paprika, curry powder and sea salt until smooth.
4. Adjust the flavour of the ketchup to be sweeter by adding another date and to be more acidic by adding a little lemon juice.
5. Add the chia seeds, mix well and leave for 15 minutes to thicken.

TIP
The chutney will store in an air tight jar in the refrigerator for up to a week. Alternatively you can freeze it in portions in an ice cube tray.

VARIATIONS
Golden berries are dried Physallis. It gives the chutney a fruity, tangy depth. You can replace this by using more lemon juice.
Place the chutney in a shallow bowl and dehydrate for 4-8 hours at 46ºC (115ºF) to intensify the flavours further.

NOTES

FOOD HEROES
TOMATOES
GARLIC

Equipment needed: dehydrator

INGREDIENTS

340g (2 cups) shelled unroasted buckwheat (makes approximately 3 cups freshly sprouted buckwheat or 2 cups buckwheaties)

water to cover

SPROUTED BUCKWHEAT/BUCKWHEATIES

Sprouted buckwheat can be eaten fresh on salads, used in recipes or dehydrated for storage, breakfasts, cakes and crackers. Once the sprouted buckwheat has been dehydrated it's called buckwheaties.

1. Rinse the buckwheat, then cover it with cold water and soak for 20-30 minutes.
2. Drain, rinse again and place the buckwheat in a sieve or nut milk bag over a bowl.
3. Cover with a clean tea towel.
4. Sprout for 24-48 hours until tiny tails emerge.
5. During this time rinse well twice daily.
6. Once the buckwheat is sprouted use in a recipe, store in the refrigerator for up to 2 days or dehydrate until crisp.

> **TIP**
> Freshly sprouted buckwheat needs to be stored in the refrigerator for no more than 2 days. Once dehydrated fully they store indefinitely in an airtight container and it's good to have them as a staple in the store cupboard.

SPROUTING SEEDS AND NUTS

Nuts and seeds contain an enzyme-inhibiting substances which prevent them from premature sprouting. However it also makes nuts and seeds harder to digest and it can interfere with the absorption of minerals. Therefore it is best to soak and 'pre-sprout' nuts and seeds such as almonds, hazelnuts, Brazil nuts, walnuts, sunflower seeds and pumpkin seeds for 8-12 hours. Soaking and sprouting 'awakens' the seed or nut and increases the amount of available nutrients. They can then be used wet, which actually makes them taste much nicer and fresher or they can be dehydrated for use in trail mixes and as a snack. Always rinse and drain nuts and seeds after soaking

FOOD HEROES

BUCKWHEAT

SMOKY SEEDS

One of the staples in our house are sprouted, dehydrated and spiced seeds. We sprinkle them on vegetable noodles, salads and soups or eat them as a snack.

Serves: 600g
Equipment needed: dehydrator
Plan ahead: requires pre-soaking and dehydrating

IINGREDIENTS

260g (2 cups) sunflower seeds, soaked 8-12 hours

280g (2 cups) pumpkin seeds, soaked 8-12 hours

65g (½ cup) sesame seeds, soaked 8-12 hours

4 tablespoons Tamari

3 teaspoons smoked paprika

2 teaspoons sweet paprika

2 teaspoons ground cumin

½ teaspoon chilli powder

1. Rinse and drain the soaked seeds.
2. Add the Tamari, smoked paprika, sweet paprika, ground cumin and mix well.
3. Add chilli powder to taste.
4. Leave to marinate for 15-30 minutes.
5. Spread onto non-stick dehydrator sheets and dehydrate for 8-16 hours at no more than 46ºC (115ºF) or until completely dry and crisp.
6. Store in an airtight container for up to 3 months.

TIP
Make up your own favourite flavour by experimenting with different spices.

NOTES

FOOD HEROES
SEEDS
SPICES

SPICY CURRY SEEDS

Serves: 600g
Equipment needed: dehydrator
Plan ahead: requires pre-soaking and dehydrating

INGREDIENTS

260g (2 cups) sunflower seeds, soaked 8-12 hours

280g (2 cups) pumpkin seeds, soaked 8-12 hours

3 teaspoons Garam Massala

2 teaspoons garlic powder

1 teaspoon curry powder

1 teaspoon sea salt

½ teaspoon cayenne

This is a variation on the recipe on page 109. I like to use different flavours for our seeds to create variety.

1. Rinse and drain the soaked seeds.
2. Add Garam Massala, garlic powder, curry powder and sea salt and mix well.
3. Add cayenne pepper to taste.
4. Spread onto non-stick dehydrator sheets and dehydrate for 8-16 hours at no more than 46ºC (115ºF) or until completely dry and crisp.
5. Store in an airtight container for up to 3 months.

TIP
Leave out the cayenne pepper or use more of it depending on your preference for spiciness.

NOTES

FOOD HEROES
SEEDS
SPICES

NUT & SEED 'PARMESAN'

Serves: approximately 350g
Equipment needed: blender or food processor

INGREDIENTS

130g (1 cup) sunflower seeds

80g (½ cup) linseeds/flax seeds

70g (½ cup) almonds

50g (½ cup) walnuts

2 tablespoons nutritional yeast flakes (optional)

1 teaspoon garlic powder

¼ teaspoon Herbamare or sea salt

I use this dairy free 'Parmesan' on both my Rawsagne and the Courgette Spirals with Tomato Sauce recipes. But it's also good sprinkled on a salad, on slices of avocado, on soups or basically wherever you want to add a bit more flavour interest. It's best made fresh but will store well in the refrigerator for up to a week.

1. Place the sunflower seeds, linseeds, almonds, walnuts, nutritional yeast flakes, garlic powder and Herbamare into a blender.
2. Pulse a few times until the nuts and seeds are ground down into a crunchy sprinkle.
3. Store in a glass jar in the refrigerator for up to a week.

VARIATION
For a completely white parmesan, use 330g blanched almonds only. Play around with different nut and seed combinations until you've created your personal favourite Nut Parmesan. Herbamare is a mix of sea salt and dried herbs and can be purchased in most healthfood shops.

NOTES

FOOD HEROES

SEEDS
NUTS
GARLIC

PINE NUT 'PARMESAN' FLAKES

Serves: 250g
Equipment needed: blender, dehydrator
Plan ahead: dehydrating

INGREDIENTS

250g (2 cups) pine nuts

125ml (½ cup) water

1 lemon, juiced

1 teaspoon sea salt

½ teaspoon pro-biotic powder

a pinch of ground turmeric

For a really luxurious finish to your pizza, vegetable noodle dish or salad, pine nut 'parmesan' flakes are just the thing. A bit more labour intensive to make, these are for special occasions.

1. Place the pine nuts, water, lemon juice, sea salt, pro-biotic powder and turmeric into a blender.
2. Blend on high speed for approximately 2 minutes to create a smooth cream.
3. Leave to ferment in a bowl at room temperature for 12-16 hours depending on how 'cheesy' you want the flavour.
4. Pour the fermented mix onto a non-stick dehydrator sheet and spread it out as thinly as you can with a spatula.
5. Dehydrate at 52ºC (125ºF) for 1 hour, followed by 4 hours at 46ºC (115ºF).
6. Carefully flip sheet onto a second non-stick dehydrator sheet and dehydrate for a further 8-10 hours or until completely dry.
7. Break the 'parmesan' into flakes, leave to cool and store in an airtight container in the refrigerator.

TIP

Pine nuts go rancid quickly, to avoid this I keep my pine nuts in the freezer. For the same reason this 'parmesan' needs to be stored in the refrigerator. Use it within a week, because it will have a tendency to go stale.

NOTES

FOOD HEROES

NUTS

CRANBERRY RELISH

Serves: 600g
Equipment needed: blender or food processor, dehydrator (optional)
Plan ahead: requires pre-soaking

INGREDIENTS

250g (2 cups) fresh or from frozen cranberries

1 orange

1 small shallot (or half if they're big)

1 pomegranate, seeds only

1 tablespoon extra virgin olive oil

¼ teaspoon sea salt

1 teaspoon agar agar

3 tablespoons water

This lovely and fresh cranberry sauce goes well with nut roasts or mushroom steaks.

1. Defrost the cranberries if you use frozen.
2. Cut the skin including the white off the orange with a sharp knife.
3. Chop orange into small chunks.
4. Place the orange pieces, cranberries, shallot, pomegranate seeds, olive oil and sea salt into a blender and pulse several times into a puree.
5. Dissolve the agar agar in hot water and simmer on a low heat for a few minutes until the agar agar is completely dissolved.
6. Pour the agar agar into the cranberry puree and blend again to mix it well.
7. Fill the fruit puree into clean, sterilised glass jars and keep it in the refrigerator for up to a week.

TIP
If you have a lot of cranberries, it makes sense to double the recipe. Freeze the finished puree in small glass jars or in an ice cube tray to create even smaller portions. Once the purée is frozen in the ice cube tray, transfer them to a freezer bag or container. This will store for 3-4 months in the freezer.

NOTES

FOOD HEROES
CRANBERRIES
ONION

NUT OR SEED MILK

Serves: makes approx. 1L nut milk
Equipment needed: blender, nut milk bag
Plan ahead: requires pre-soaking

INGREDIENTS

130g (1 cup) nuts or seeds, soaked for 8-12 hours
750ml (3 cups) filtered or spring water

Nut milks are a great alternative to dairy milk and are a better option than bought nut milks which are not raw and often contain sugar and other additives. Use nut milk in tea, coffee, on breakfast cereals, to make 'hot chocolate' drinks and for use in recipes.

1. Rinse and drain the nuts or seeds.
2. Blend the nuts with the water for 1-2 minutes on high speed.
3. Strain the liquid through a nut milk bag into a large jar, squeezing the bag to extract as much of the milk as possible.
4. You will be left with dry pulp which can be used in cracker and cake recipes.
5. Keep the milk in a glass bottle in the refrigerator for up to 3 days.

VARIATIONS

Hazelnuts, almonds, pumpkin seeds, sesame seeds, sunflower seeds, hemp seeds or Brazil nuts are all good options for nut milk. Find your favourite flavour.

NOTES

FOOD HEROES

NUTS

CASHEW CREAM

Serves: makes approx. 600ml
Equipment needed: blender
Plan ahead: requires pre-soaking

INGREDIENTS

260g (2 cups) cashews soaked for 30 minutes, rinsed and drained

350ml (1½ cups) filtered water

Cashew cream is extremely versatile as you can flavour it sweet or savoury.

1. Blend cashews and water until smooth and creamy.
2. Store in glass jars in the refrigerator for 2-3 days.

TIP
To save time, make double the amount and freeze the cream in smaller portions. Add flavours like cinnamon, cacao, herbs, garlic, lemon, natural sweeteners etc.

VARIATION
Try different nuts and seeds. Sunflower seeds are delicious but you won't get a white cream. Try blanched almonds or macadamia nuts, both need to be soaked over night, and you will need a very powerful blender.

NOTES

FOOD HEROES
NUTS

CASHEW YOGHURT

Serves: makes approx. 600ml yoghurt
Equipment needed: blender,
Plan ahead: requires pre-soaking and fermenting

260g (2 cups) cashews soaked for 30 minutes, rinsed and drained

350ml (1½ cups) filtered water

¼ teaspoon pro-biotic powder, lactose free

Cashew yoghurt is easy to make and versatile. Use it as a topping on fruit salad, breakfast puddings or as a base for savoury dressings.

1. Blend cashews, water and pro-biotic powder until smooth and creamy (approximately 2 minutes).
2. Pour the cream into a large glass jar and cover the top lightly with the screw top.
3. Keep at room temperature to ferment for 12-16 hours.
4. Once the yoghurt has fermented tighten the screw top and keep it in the refrigerator for up to one week.

VARIATIONS

You can also make yoghurt with sunflower seeds, but you won't get the lovely white colour. Soak sunflower seeds for 8-12 hours. Rinse and drain and then blend in the same proportions as for cashew yoghurt.

NOTES

FOOD HEROES

NUTS

BASIC MACADAMIA NUT 'CHEESE'

Equipment needed: blender

Plan ahead: requires pre-soaking and fermenting

INGREDIENTS

260g (2 cups) macadamia nuts, soaked for 20 minutes

250ml (1 cup) filtered water

1 teaspoon dairy/lactose free pro-biotic powder

2 tablespoons nutritional yeast flakes (optional)

¼ teaspoon sea salt

Nut and seed cheeses are a great alternative to dairy cheese and are used in various recipes. They are also very tasty as a spread on crackers or in a vegetable wrap. I could write a book on making nut cheeses, but for now use this as a starting point and experiment with flavours!

1. Rinse and drain the macadamia nuts.
2. Blend the nuts with the water and pro-biotic powder for 1-2 minutes into a smooth paste.
3. Spoon the mixture into a nut milk bag or cheese cloth and place it into a sieve that sits on a bowl.
4. Wrap the cheese well and sit a heavy jar on top (coconut oil jars are perfect for this purpose).
5. Cover the cheese and jar with a clean tea towel and leave to ferment at room temperature for up to 48 hours. Taste the cheese every 12 hours until the mix has a cheesy flavour.
6. Remove the cheese from the nut milk bag/cheese cloth and place into a clean bowl.
7. Add the yeast flakes and sea salt and mix well.
8. Store the cheese in an airtight container in the refrigerator for up to 2 weeks.

VARIATIONS

Any nut or seed can be fermented. Add spices or herbs to create different flavour cheese spreads. You can shape the mix into a round cheese, wrap it in grease proof paper and let it mature in the refrigerator. It will get dryer and develop a crust. Experiment!

NOTES

FOOD HEROES

NUTS

3 tablespoons raw cider vinegar

1 teaspoon coconut sugar

1 thumb ginger

PICKLED GINGER

A great way to use and store fresh ginger. Use it on salads and in wraps.

1. Disolve the coconut sugar in the cider vinegar.
2. Peel the ginger and slice it as thin as you can (you're aiming for paper-thin!).
3. Place the ginger into a small glass jar with a screw top lid and cover it with the vinegar solution.
4. Leave the ginger to marinate for at least 1 hour, the longer the better.

VARIATIONS
Try the same recipe using fresh turmeric.

TIP
Pickled ginger will store in the refrigerator for many weeks. You can even top it up with fresh ginger if the jar still contains enough vinegar solution.

NOTES

FOOD HEROES
GINGER

FOOD
HEROES

LEAFY GREENS

Broccoli

A member of the cruciferous family and, along with cauliflower, one of which we eat the flower head rather than the leaves.

Broccoli is an excellent source of chromium, vitamins C, K and folic acid. It is also a very good source of copper, manganese, phosphorus, potassium, vitamins B2, B6, E and fibre and a good source of calcium, iron, magnesium, selenium, zinc, vitamin B1, protein and essential fatty acids.

Phytonutrients

Broccoli contains the phytonutrients carotenoids (lutein and zeaxanthin), glucosinolates (lucoraphanin, gluconasturtiian, glucobrassicin) and flavonoids (kaempferol)

Unique Health Benefits

The combination of vitamin E, manganese, zinc and flavonoids make broccoli a star antioxidant vegetable, reducing inflammation and cancer risk. The unique combination of glucosinolates in broccoli support liver detoxification pathways through indole-3-carbinol and sulforaphane and increase the excretion of oestrogens linked to breast cancer[1]. Research suggests that sulforaphane may also be useful against rheumatoid arthritis[2], as well as other cancers through its detoxification properties and its ability to modulate cell death[3]. Sulfuraphane may also help counteract sun damage to skin[4]. Lutein is concentrated in the retina so along with its anti-cancer properties, it may also be helpful in preventing the development of age-related macular degeneration[5].

Caution

Broccoli is high in isothiocyanates and as such, any individual with a diagnosed under-active thyroid would be better cooking broccoli lightly, which deactivates this chemical compound that can have a thyroid suppressive effect.

Kale & cabbage

A cruciferous vegetable closely related to cabbage, broccoli, Brussels sprouts, cauliflower etc. While we mainly use the flower head of broccoli and cauliflower, we eat the leaves of kale and cabbage, so their nutritional profiles are a bit different.

Kale and cabbages are an excellent source of: copper, manganese, Pro-vitamin A, vitamin C and K. It is also a very good source of calcium, potassium, vitamins B2, B6, E and fibre. Kale and cabbages are a good source of iron, magnesium, phosphorous, vitamins B1, B3, folate and omega 3 fatty acids.

Phytonutrients

They contain the phytonutrients glucosinolates (including sinigrin), polyphenols (particularly anthocyanins in red cabbage), carotenoids (lutein and beta-carotene), flavonoids (a range of over 40, including kaempferol, quercetin)

Unique Health Benefits

Kale and cabbage, like broccoli, are very high in glucosinolates with demonstrable anti-cancer properties through their ability to detoxify and eliminate harmful chemicals and their antioxidant action. Cabbage juice has traditionally been used as a successful treatment for peptic ulcers and the active ingredient is often referred to as 'vitamin U'.

Caution

As for broccoli regarding thyroid.

For full references visit www.gabrielalerner.com/p/references

Romaine Lettuce

Romaine lettuce is one of the salads with the most nutritious value. It is an excellent source of vitamins K, A, folate and molybdenum and a very good source of manganese, potassium, copper, iron and fibre as well as biotin, vitamin B1 and C.

Spinach

Spinach belongs to the same family as beets and chard – and when you buy fresh beetroot the leaves can be used in exactly the same way as spinach. Spinach contains twice as much iron as most other green vegetables and is one of the most alkalising.

Spinach is an excellent source of vitamins K, C and folic acid. It's a good source of manganese, magnesium, iron and vitamin B2.

Phytonutrients

Spinach is one of the richest sources of the carotenoid lutein, which promotes eye health and may be helpful in preventing the development of age-related macular degeneration. There appear to be no less than 13 different flavonoid compounds to be found in spinach that function as antioxidants and anticancer agents. Spinach extract has been shown to slow down the division rate of cancer cells.[6]

Caution

Spinach contains high levels of oxalates which can cause problems through crystallisation. Therefore individuals with existing kidney or gall bladder problems should avoid eating too much spinach.

Watercress

Watercress is not always recognised as a cruciferous vegetable family, but it has all the benefits of the other family members. It is rich in vitamins K, A and C and beta-carotene.

Phytonutrients

It's an excellent source of the carotenoid, lutein as well as ze-axanthin, both of which are linked to a lower risk of age-related macular degeneration and protection from skin cancers[7]. Studies also suggest that lutein is protective of the cardiovascular system[8].

ROOTS & BULBS

Beets

Beetroot are part of the same family as spinach and both the leaves and the root can be eaten. The leaves have much the same nutritional profile as chard and spinach and here we are discussing the nutritional benefits of the root. The root portion of beets provide a good source of energy through the carbohydrate content, mainly as sugars.

As you can see from the health benefits below, beetroot are real superfoods and should be included in your diet on a very regular basis. They are an excellent source of folic acid and a very good source of manganese, potassium and copper. They are also a good source of vitamin C and B6, magnesium, iron and fibre

Phytonutrients

Beets contain two types of betalains (betaxanthins and betacyanins), the chemicals that give beetroot their strong colours. These function as both antioxidants and anti-inflammatory molecules. These chemicals are not readily found in other vegetables (although red chard and rhubarb are both sources) and they appear to be responsible for some of the unique properties of beetroot.

Roots are the energy stores for the plant and therefore they are also great energy providers for us.

Unique Health Benefits

Research suggests that beetroot reduce inflammation by inhibiting the same inflammatory pathways targeted by aspirin[9]. Beetroot helps potentiate liver detoxification through the increase of the level of specific antioxidant enzymes. The combination of antioxidant properties and soluble fibre makes beets a potent tool for the prevention of stomach and colon cancer[10]. The fibre has been shown to be beneficial for bowel function and cholesterol levels. Betaine is a key nutrient for regulating methylation pathways that have been shown to affect cardiovascular health[11] and DNA replication[12].

Caution

Eating beetroot can cause beeturia (pink or red colour in the urine), which is generally not considered harmful. However, this is known to be more prevalent if you have problems with iron metabolism and it would be worth checking your iron levels if you do experience beeturia.

Carrots

An excellent source of pro-vitamin A (in the form of beta-carotene) – which means we can make our own vitamin A from beta-carotene. A very good source of vitamins B2, B6, C and K, and the minerals molybdenum and potassium. Carrots are also a good source of vitamins B1, B2, B3, B5, folic acid and E as well as copper, manganese, phosphorus and dietary fibre.

Phytonutrients

Carrots contain the phytonutrients carotenoids (including alpha and beta-carotene and lutein). Light cooking can help release the carotenoids making them easier to absorb. Hydroxycinnamic acids (including caffeic, coumaric and ferulic acids) and polyacetylenes (including falcarinol and falcarindiol)

Unique health benefits

Lutein is closely connected to eye health (see broccoli). Polyacetylenes have been shown to be anti-inflammatory and anti-clumping (which means they stop red blood cells from clogging together).[13] A recent 10-year study at Wageningen University in the Netherlands has shown that carrots have remarkable cardiovascular protective properties, even over other sources of carotenoids. 25g of carrots daily provided a significantly reduced risk of cardiovascular disease.

Soluble fibre protects the colon from cancer and works as a 'pre-biotic', which means it provides nourishment for our gut bacteria. Evidence suggests a strong link between carotenoids and cancer prevention, particularly breast cancer[14]

Caution

Carrots have been found to have some of the highest levels of pesticide residues, so best to choose organic.

Fennel

Fennel is a bulb rather than a root, which means the fibre contains more cellulose than the soluble pectin found in carrots and beetroot. The bulb, stems, leaves and seeds are all edible.It is an excellent source vitamin C, a very good source of copper, manganese, molybdenum, phosphorus, folate and fibre, as well as a good source of calcium, magnesium and vitamin B3.

Phytonutrients

Flavonoids (including rutin and quercetin), kaempferol glycosides and anethole.

Unique health benefits

Rutin and quercetin are known to enhance the action of vitamin C, particularly in the formation of healthy collagen, so useful for maintaining strong blood vessels. Quercetin and rutin have been shown to modify inflammation, protect from damage to the fats in our blood and from platelet aggregation, therefore maintaining a healthy cardiovascular system[15]. They can also reduce the pain of neuropathy[16]. Kaempferol glycosides give fennel a huge range of antioxidant properties, including anti-cancer, cardio-protective, anti-inflammatory and anti-microbial[17]. Anethole is not a widely recognised antioxidant (it is the chief constituent of the volatile oils in camphor, anise and fennel) but exciting research is beginning to reveal that it has strong anti-cancer properties (particularly for breast cancer) and for regulating inflammatory pathways.[18,19]

Onion

Onions are bulbs and are one of the most nutrient-packed vegetable around with the added benefit of not being expensive and being available all year round. We would be doing ourselves a big favour by having a helping every day. Onions, leeks and garlic are all members of the allium family and it is the health-promoting sulphur compounds in this family of foods that gives them their pungent flavour.

Onions are a very good source of vitamin B2, a good source of vitamins B1, B6 and C, folate, copper, manganese, phosphorous and potassium.

Phytonutrients
Onions are really high in the phytonutrients polyphenols, including flavonoids and quercetin in particular. The sulphides found in onions make them particularly useful for detoxification pathways.

Unique health benefits
Less well researched than garlic, onion also has anti-bacterial properties and these benefits may include protection against gum disease[20]. Raw, freshly prepared onion demonstrated these effects, not shown in cooked onions.

Sweet potato

Sweet potatoes are an excellent source of pro-vitamin A (in the form of beta-carotene), a very good source of vitamins B5, B6 and C, as well as copper and manganese. They are also a good source of the vitamins biotin, B1, B2 and B3, phosphorus, potassium and fibre.

Phytonutrients
Sweet Potatoes contain the phytonutrients anthocyanins (including peonidins and cyanidins), batatins, batatosides and sporamins

Unique health benefits
Excellent for balancing blood sugars, even for type II diabetics, due to the action of a protein hormone called adiponectin. This molecule is critical for modifying insulin metabolism and is not typically found in other root vegetables.[21] The anthocyanins found in purple fleshed sweet potatoes provide antioxidant protection and are effective at removing damaging heavy metal residues in the diet. They also have a protective effect on nerve cells and the damage from excess fibrin. Batatins have anti-microbial and anti-fungal properties and it will be interesting to see if research finds these benefits are conferred to our digestive tract, giving sweet potato a role in balancing gut bacteria and yeast overgrowth. Sporamins are storage proteins that heal any damage to the sweet potato tuber itself and when eaten this protective action is transferred to our own cells, particularly those of the gut[22].

Caution
Sweet potatoes are deemed to be high in oxalates (although much lower than spinach) and therefore individuals with existing kidney or gall bladder problems should avoid eating too many sweet potatoes.

For full references visit www.gabrielalerner.com/p/references

SALADS

Celery

All parts of the celery may be eaten, stalks, leaves, flowers and seeds. The seeds make an excellent alternative to salt for flavouring.

Celery is an excellent source of the mineral molybdenum and vitamin K, a very good source of manganese, potassium, vitamin B5, folate, and fibre. It is also a good source of calcium, copper, magnesium, phosphorous and the vitamins A, B2, B6 and C

Phytonutrients
Celery contains flavonoids (apigenin and luteolin), pthalides, coumarins and apiuman.

Unique health benefits
The mineral balance of celery makes celery juice an excellent electrolyte replacement after a workout. Traditionally celery has been used to relieve the pain of gout, probably due to the diuretic effect of phthalides (3nB). These compounds also appear to help relax smooth muscle, particularly in the cardiovascular system, so can reduce blood pressure. Apigenin has anti-cancer and anti-inflammatory properties[23]. Luteolin effectively maintains healthy methylation pathways that protect us fro DNA mutations. It has been shown to switch off pathways that lead to inflammation in the brain and is protective against tumour formation and proliferation[24]. The pectin-based polysaccharides found in celery, particularly apiuman, appear to have special anti-inflammatory benefits. Extracts have been shown to improve the integrity of the stomach lining, control gastric secretions and decrease the risk of gastric ulcers [25].

For full references visit www.gabrielalerner.com/p/references

Caution
For some individuals with a birch allergy there is the possibility of cross reactivity with celery, so you may want to check if this may affect you, however it is relatively rare. Conventionally grown celery can be high in pesticide residue, so best to buy organic celery.

Cucumber

Cucumbers are an excellent source of the mineral molybdenum and vitamin K. They are also a very good source of vitamin B5 and a good source of the minerals copper, magnesium, manganese and phosphorous and vitamins B1, C and biotin.

Phytonutrients
Cucumbers contain flavonoids, including apigenin, luleolin, quercetin and kaempferol, lignans, including lariciresinol, pinoresinol and secoisolariciresinol and triterpenes, including cucurbitacins A, B, C and D.

Unique health benefits
The health benefits of the flavonoids in cucumber have been discussed elsewhere. The three lignans in cucumber have been researched in connection with reducing the risk of cardiovascular disease and several types of cancer. They are converted into 'enterolignans' by our gut bacteria and have the ability to balance oestrogen levels, reducing the risk of oestrogen-related cancers.[26, 27] Triterpenes have the ability to block cancer cell development and therefore give cucumbers a cancer protective benefit[28].

Caution
Conventionally grown cucumbers can be high in pesticide residues and may also be waxed with synthetic waxes and other compounds to protect them. To avoid these it is better to buy organically grown cucumbers.

Peppers

Peppers are an excellent source of the vitamins B6 and C and pro-vitamin A. They are a very good source of the minerals molybdenum and potassium, the vitamins B2, B3, B5, E, folate and fibre. Peppers are a good source of magnesium, manganese, phosphorous and vitamin B1 and K.

Phytonutrients

Peppers contain flavonoids (luteolin, quercetin, hesperidin), carotenoids – over 30 different carotenoids, including alpha and beta carotene, cryptoxanthin, lutein, zeaxanthin and hydroxycinnamic acids (ferulic acid, cinnamic acid).

Unique health benefits

The combination of lutein and zeaxanthin provide potent eye protection, particularly from age-related macular degeneration[29]. The broad range of antioxidant phytonutrients suggest that peppers provide wide scope for protection from cancer and oxidative stress.Peppers increase their nutrient profile as they reach optimum ripeness and will continue to improve their levels of vitamin C and carotenoids even while ripening in your kitchen.

Caution

Peppers are often high in pesticide residues and therefore it may be better to buy organically grown. Peppers are members of the nightshade family and should be avoided by those with a sensitivity to this group of foods.

Tomatoes

Tomatoes are an excellent source of molybdenum, biotin and vitamin C a very good source of manganese, phosphorous, potassium, vitamin B3, B6, E, folate, pro-vitamin A and fibre.

They are also a good source of chromium, iron, magnesium, zinc the vitamins B1, B5 choline

Phytonutrients

Tomatoes contain flavonones (narignenin, chalconaringenin), flavonoids (rutin, kaempferol, quercetin), hydroxycinnamic acids (caffeic acid, ferulic acid, coumaric acid), carotenoids (lycopene, lutein, zeaxanthin, beta-carotene) and glycosides (saponins).

Unique health benefits

The combination of high levels of the important antioxidant vitamins C and E and the huge array of antioxidants makes tomatoes (both red and yellow) king of the cardiovascular support group. Not only can tomatoes protect circulating fats from damage they can help regulate cholesterol.[30,31,32]
Lycopene has also been found to improve bone density, a benefit that appears to be linked to its antioxidant protection[33].
Tomatoes are probably best known for their links with prostate cancer protection and there is on-going research into possible benefits for other cancers, including certain lung cancers, breast cancer and pancreatic cancer[34].

Caution

Tomatoes are often high in pesticide residues and therefore it may be better to buy organically grown.Tomatoes are members of the nightshade family and should be avoided by those with a sensitivity to this group of foods.

FRUITS

Apples

The well-known saying may have its foundations in truth – as we learn more about the unique balance of phytonutrients found in an apple we understand how it has equally unique health benefits. Most of the phytonutrients are concentrated in the skin, particularly quercetin and anthocyanins in red-skinned apples, and it seems that these are concentrated there to protect the apples themselves from UV-B light damage, in other words, they are a natural sun screen.

Apples are a good source of vitamin C, fibre, particularly the soluble fibre pectin.

Phytonutrients

Apples contain flavonoids (quercetin in particular, daempferol, myrecetin), catechins (epicatechin) and anthocyanins (only found in the skin of red skinned apples).

Unique health benefits

The combination of soluble fibre and antioxidants are particularly protective of the cardiovascular system and protective against cancers, particularly lung cancer.[35, 36] Apples seem to be uniquely strongly protective against asthma, as a result of the high levels of quercetin[37].

Avocado

A tree fruit that is high in the fatty alcohols normally only found in algae and ocean plants.

Avocados are a good source of copper, potassium, vitamins B5, B6, C, E, folate, K and fibre.

Phytonutrients

Avocados contain phytosterols, carotenoids (including the less common neoxanthin, neochrome, chrysanthemaxannthin, beta-cryptoxanthin, violaxanthin and alpha-carotene), omega 3 fatty acids and polyhydroxylated fatty alcohols

Unique health benefits

The combination of fatty acids, fatty alcohols, phytosterols and antoxidant flavonoids and carotenoids makes avocados especially anti-inflammatory, with particular benefits for both osteoarthritis and rheumatoid arthritis. The phytosterols appear to prevent the over-production of a particular pro-inflammatory compound known as prostaglandin E2[38]. Studies are beginning to show that avocados have the amazing benefit of being able to reduce oxidative damage (and thereby possible cell death) to healthy cells, while inducing programmed cell death in cancerous cells[39]. The fibre and very particular form of carbohydrate found in avocados makes them an important controller of blood sugar levels, although as they ripen the carbohydrates alter, so over-ripe avocados are not such a good choice. Choose slightly soft buy firm avocodos.

Fat soluble vitamins, carotenoids and flavonoids can only be absorbed in the presence of fats. So, bring on the avocados, not only as a fat soluble anti-oxidant boost but as a super-absorber of these nutrients from other foods. The combination of phytosterols and fatty alcohols provide significant benefits for normalising cholesterol[40].

Caution

Enzymes in avocados are associated with the latex-fruit allergy syndrome. If you have a latex allergy, you may very likely be allergic to avocados as well. Processing the fruit with ethylene gas increases these enzymes and organic produce not treated with gas will have fewer allergy-causing compounds.

Banana

Bananas are a very good source of vitamin B6 and a good source of copper, manganese, potassium, biotin, vitamin C and fibre.

Unique health benefits

The pre-biotic fibres in bananas are particularly beneficial for the gut and surprisingly for their high sugar content, bananas can improve gut health in several ways: the pectin can help ease constipation (while restoring levels of lost potassium) and the resistant starch can nourish beneficial bacteria. They are a natural antacid.

Caution

Enzymes in bananas are associated with the latex-fruit allergy syndrome. If you have a latex allergy, you may very likely be allergic to bananas as well. Processing the fruit with ethylene gas increases these enzymes and organic produce not treated with gas will have fewer allergy-causing compounds.

Berries

All berries provide significant antioxidant protection and the best way of getting this is to eat a mix of different berries as they come into season. The humble (and frequently free) blackberry can often provide the most benefit, which is very satisfying. Berries also contain many tiny seeds that can provide useful levels of essential fatty acids.

Berries are an excellent source of manganese (particularly raspberries), Vitamin C (particularly raspberries, strawberries and blackberries) and they are a very good source of iodine (particularly strawberries) and vitamin K. They are also a good source of copper, vitamin B5, biotin, vitamin E, folate (particularly raspberries and blackberries) and fibre.

Phytonutrients

Berries are rich in phytonutrients including anthocyanins, hydroxycinnamic acids, hydroxybenzoic acids, flavonoids, tannins resveratrol and pterostilbene.

Unique health benefits

The huge range of antioxidant nutrients means that berries are beneficial for pretty well every system in the body, from eyes to muscles, from neurogenerative disorders, to cardiovascular problems including blood sugar balance and cancer protection The protection of the nerve cells gives berries a leading role in protection of cognitive function and improvement of memory[41]. Berries also have a particular benefit for blood sugar management even for those already diagnosed with problems[42]. Berries may also be useful for inflammatory bowel disease[43].

Caution

Commercially grown berries are often high in pesticide residues (particularly strawberries and blueberries) and therefore it may be better to buy organically grown. Studies suggest that the total antioxidant capacity of organically grown blueberries is superior to non-organically grown berries. Berries are deemed to be high in oxalates (although much lower than spinach) and therefore individuals with existing kidney or gall bladder problems should avoid eating too many berries.

Grapes

There are many different varieties of grapes and clearly not all varieties contain all the huge variety of phytonutrients that have been identified in grapes as a whole. It is also important to remember that the highest concentration of antioxidants is found in the skin and seeds, which explains why red grapes confer a higher antioxidant benefit than white. Grapes are a very good source of copper and vitamin K and a good source of vitamin B2.

Phytonutrients

Grapes contain stilbenes, particularly resveratrol, flavanols (including catechins, epicatechins and proanthocyanidins), flavonoids (including quercetin and kaempferol), phenolic acids and caretonoids.

Unique health benefits

Grapes are remarkably high in antioxidant nutrients which means they can provide huge benefits for heart health, including blood pressure regulation, cholesterol management, less inappropriate clumping of blood cells, vasodilation and better inflammatory control. Grapes are classified as low GI and together with their resveratrol this gives grapes a role to play in improving blood sugar regulation[44]. Grapeseeds have been used for many years as an anti-fungal and anti-microbial. Studies have shown that antioxidant and anti-inflammatory properties of grape juice are beneficial for cognitive function[45]. Resveratrol has been shown to have a beneficial effect on longevity – so grapes may even have an anti-ageing effect[46].

Caution

Take care not to equate the nutritional benefit of grapes with the dried fruit. While dehydration reduces the grapes' water content it increases their concentration of sugar and calories. The result is that in every ounce of raisins, you end up getting four times the amount of sugar and calories than you would from an ounce of grapes, even though you aren't getting any more vitamins and minerals. Conventionally grown grapes are often heavily sprayed with pesticides and it's therefore best to buy organic. Also look for grapes containing seeds because of the health benefits of the seeds mentioned.

Lemons & Limes

Lemons and limes are an excellent source of vitamin C and a good source of folate.

Phytonutrients

Lemons and limes contain the limonin and the flavonoid kaempherol.

Unique health benefits

Lemons and limes both have strong anti-bacterial properties, provided by the flavonoid kaempferol. This protection is active both when the fruit and juice is ingested and also when used topically on us and our environment such as kitchen surfaces.

The flavonols in lemons and limes have been shown to potentiate the activities of monocytes, cells of our immune system that control healthy cell division or self-destruction.[47]

Mango

Mango is an excellent source of copper, vitamin C and provitamin A. It is a good source of magnesium, potassium, vitamin B, E and fibre.

Phytonutrients

Mangos contain carotenoids, flavonoids, polyphenols and enzymes.

Unique health benefits

Mango has been shown to be effective against giardia infections (commonly known as 'travellers' tummy') and certain viruses. The combination of carotenoids and possible protection from parasitic and viral infections makes mango a potentially excellent conditioner for the gastro-intestinal tract. Recent studies and on-going research suggest an important anti-cancer role for mangoes, linked to their polyphenol content[48].

Caution

Mango is distantly related to poison ivy and the skin may cause irritation, particularly if the fruit is slightly unripe.

Pineapple

Pineapple is an excellent source of manganese and vitamin C, a very good source of copper and good source of vitamin B1, B5, B6, folate and fibre.

Phytonutrients

Pineapples contain the enzyme bromelain.

Unique health benefits

Bromelain has been identified as an important enzyme for breaking down proteins and this can have a benefit for digestion as well as for reducing inflammation. Whether or not the amount of Bromelain in pineapple can be therapeutically beneficial has not yet been established but it seems probable that the core of the pineapple may provide the greatest health benefits. Interestingly, it appears that pineapples use their bromelain reserves in their stems as an enzyme to break down nutrients from debris that falls into the rainwater reservoirs made by their leaves.

Pomegranate

A fruit derived from a small tree, grown originally in Iran and used frequently in traditional savoury Persian recipes. Now widely cultivated world wide. The whole fruit provides the best nutrients because both the seeds and the red, juicy flesh are eaten. Pomegranates are widely used in Ayurvedic medicine.

Pomegranates are an excellent source of the vitamins C and K and a very good source of fibre.

Phytonutrients

Pomegranate contains the polyphenols tannins and anthcyanins.

Unique health benefits

Research suggests pomegranate exert particular benefits on the cardiovascular system by reducing damage from oxidative stress,[49] lowering blood pressure,[50] supporting nitric oxide synthesis[51] and inhibiting the oxidation of LDL making it potentially harmful. They also appear to have benefits for diabetes[52] and support liver function[53].

HERBS & SPICES

Coriander

In the same plant family as parsley, we commonly eat both the seeds and leaves of coriander and as we would expect, each part brings different nutritional benefit. It is an excellent source of vitamin K (leaves), a good source of calcium, copper, iron, magnesium, manganese (seeds) vitamin C and pro-vitamin A.

Phytonutrients

Coriander contains flavonoids (including quercetin and kaempferol), phenolic acids (include caffeic and chlorogenic acid).

Unique health benefits

Coriander appears to have antibiotic and anti-microbial properties through dodecenal. It could therefore be useful against fungal, bacterial and yeast infections, including salmonella, which is pretty impressive[48]. Coriander can also be useful as a heavy metal detoxifier.

Garlic

Like onions, garlic is a member of the allium family and high in the same sulphur related phytonutrients. Garlic is an excellent source of manganese and vitamin B6, a very good source of copper and vitamin C and a good source of calcium, phosphorus, selenium and vitamin B1.

Phytonutrients

Garlic contains many sulphur containing nutrients.

Unique health benefits

The health benefits of garlic are legendary (literally) and include its antibacterial, anti-microbial and antiviral properties. The sulphur compounds can help dilate blood vessels and keep blood pressure under control[49]. These same compounds protect our cardiovascular system from oxidative stress and inflammation, both of which can cause damage to blood vessels[50]. Garlic can also help prevent the formation of blood clots – so it is all round a super heart-protective food[51]. A recent study showed that garlic was remarkably effective at treating warts[52]. Garlic also helps to release iron from storage and into circulation for use.

Ginger

An extremely versatile spice used in savoury and sweet foods s well as drinks. The part of the plant that we use is the under-ground rhizome.

Phytonutrients

Ginger's health benefits appear to derive from the various unique gingerol phenolic constituents.

Unique health benefits

It is safe to use during pregnancy for nausea and vomiting and can be very effective[53]. Gingerols are potent anti-inflammatory compounds making ginger an effective treatment for the pain of both rheumatoid and osteoarthritis[54]. Gingerols may also have a chemo-protective effect, particularly for colorectal cancer and ovarian cancer[55].

Parsley

So much more than just a garnish, parsley is packed with goodness, so use it liberally in your meals. Thanks to its long tap root it can obtain minerals from deep in the soil, which accounts for the mineral content of its leaves.

Parsley is an excellent source of iron, vitamins A (as pro-vitamin A beta-carotene), vitamin C and folate. It is a very good source of copper and a good source of calcium, magnesium, manganese, phosphorous, potassium, zinc and the vitamins B1 and B3.

Phytonutrients

Parsley contains volatile oil including limonene and myristicin and flavonoids including apigenin and luteolin.

Unique health benefits

The volatile oils give parsley its chemo-protective properties, particularly against lung tumours[56]. The antioxidant flavonoids apigenin and luteolin prevent cell damage from oxygen radicals[57]. Some studies suggest an important role for parsley in healthy kidney function[58].

Rosemary

Traditionally known as the herb for memory, we now know that rosemary increases the blood flow to the head and brain so may well enhance memory and concentration through this[59].

Unique health benefits

The volatile oils in rosemary can help stimulate circulation. Rosemary can have a toning and calming effect on digestion. One study suggests the antioxidant properties of rosemary can inhibit lung inflammation[60].

For full references visit www.gabrielalerner.com/p/references

Turmeric

A traditional spice in Indian cookery and Chinese and Indian medicines, in the west we are finally acknowledging the health benefits of turmeric for us all.

Unique health benefits

Curcumin is the primary active ingredient in turmeric and gives the root its distinctive colour. It has powerful anti-inflammatory properties with none of the toxic side effects of comparable drugs. The anti-inflammatory properties of turmeric include benefits for IBD, rheumatoid arthritis and prevention of several forms of cancer. One study suggests curcumin can correct the genetic defect responsible for cystic fibrosis[61].

NUTS & SEEDS

Nuts and seeds are best if soaked overnight or at least a few hours. This soaking removes some of the enzyme inhibitors that naturally protects the nut or seed from sprouting prematurely. Removing the enzyme inhibitors releases their enzymes, making them easier to digest and their nutrients more available to the body.

Almonds

Like all nuts, almonds are high in beneficial monounsaturated fats that have been shown to lower cholesterol when eaten in preference to saturated animal fats.

Almonds are a very good source of the vitamins biotin, B2 and E, as well as the mineral copper. It is also a good source of vitamin B2 and magnesium, molybdenum and phosphorus.

Phytonutrients

Almonds contain the phytonutrients catechins and flavonols, which are found predominantly in the skin.

Unique health benefits

Almonds are particularly good for cardiovascular health – but you need to include the skins for the most benefit as the flavonoids in the skin act in synergy with the vitamin E1.

Buckwheat

Buckwheat is not a grain and can therefore be a suitable substitute for those with grain sensitivities. It is in fact a seed related to rhubarb.

Buckwheat is a very good source of manganese and contains all essential amino acids, making it a valuable protein source. It is also a good source of copper, magnesium and phosphorus.

Phytonutrients

Buckwheat contains flavonoids, particularly rutin that has been linked to the protection of cognitive impairment[69], and is also cardioprotective[70].

Chia Seeds

The word 'Chia' comes from the Mayan language and means strength. The balance of protein, carbohydrates, fats and fibre gives chia its reputation as the 'perfect' superfood and it is said that one tablespoon of Chia can sustain a person for 24 hours.

Chia is an excellent source of omega 3 fatty acids, the minerals calcium, magnesium, manganese and phosphorus, as well as fibre and protein. It is a good source of the vitamins B1, B2, B3, and the minerals potassium and zinc.

Phytonutrients

Chia contains the phytonutrients quercetin, kaempferol, chlorogenic acid, and caffeic acid

Unique health benefits

The antioxidants found in chia seeds are naturally focused on protecting the fats in the seed itself and they can convey these benefits to us. They have been shown to reduce the size of carcinogenic tumours[71], improve the blood sugar balance of diabetics[72] and protect the cardiovascular system from damage, particularly post stroke[73].

Flax (Linseeds)

Flax is an excellent source of omega 3 fatty acids and a very good source of vitamin B1, copper and manganese.

It is also a good source of magnesium, phosphorus and selenium.

Unique health benefits

The antioxidant and anti-inflammatory properties of flaxseeds are particularly linked to decreasing the risk of insulin resistance, type 2 diabetes, obesity and metabolic syndrome[74].

Hazelnuts

Hazelnuts are an excellent source of omega 6 essential fatty acids and vitamin E, as well as manganese.

They are also a very good source of the minerals copper, magnesium and phosphorus, and fibre. Hazelnuts are a good source of the vitamins B6 and folic alic.

Phytonutrients

Hazelnuts contain flavonoids, proanthocyanidins and phytosterols.

Unique health benefits

The high levels of phytosterols make hazelnuts particularly effective for lowering cholesterol[75].

Hemp Seeds

Hemp seeds are an excellent mix of fats (one-third) and complete protein (one-quarter). They have an excellent 3:1 balance of omega 3 and 6 essential fatty acids. Hemp is a good source of vitamin E.

Unique health benefits

Because hemp seeds contain all the essential amino acids, they are an excellent source of vegetarian protein. The balance of fatty acids make hempseeds useful for inflammatory conditions such as rheumatoid arthritis[76].

Pumpkin Seeds

Pumpkin seeds are a very good source of copper, magnesium, manganese, and phosphorus, and a good source of iron and zinc. They also contain good amounts of protein.

Phytonutrients

Pumkin seeds contain a wide variety of antioxidant phytonutrients including phenolic acids and lignans.

Sunflower Seeds

Sunflower seeds are an excellent source of vitamin E and a very good source of vitamin B1, copper, as well as a good source of the vitamins B3, B6 and folate, and the minerals magnesium, manganese, phosphorus and selenium.

Unique health benefits

The phytosterol compounds found in sunflower seeds have a similar structure to our own cholesterol and are beneficial for maintaining healthy cholesterol levels in the blood.[77]

Walnuts

Walnuts are an excellent source of omega 3 and 6 fatty acids. They are also a very good source of copper manganese, and a good source of the mineral molybdenum and the vitamin biotin.

Phytonutrients

Walnuts contain forms of important phytonutrients, such as quinone, juglone, the tannin tellimagrandin and the flavonol morin, that are rarely found in other commonly-eaten foods.

Unique health benefits

The form of vitamin E in walnuts makes them specifically beneficial for cardiovascular health. Walnuts consumption has been shown to reduce the risk of both prostate[78] and breast cancers.

SEAGREENS

Kelp, Nori, Wakame, Hijiki, Dulse, Sea Spaghetti

Seagreens are increasingly becoming part of the western diet and they are a rich source of iodine and probably vanadium (this conjecture is due to its high levels of vanadium dependent enzymes). There is debate about the source of seagreens, due to the possibility of arsenic pollution. Certified organic vegetables will reduce this risk and it is always important to remember the benefit to risk ratio of all healthy foods that may contain pollutants.

Seagreens are an excellent source of vitamins B2 and C, and the minerals Iodine and manganese. They are a very good source of vitamin A, copper and a good source of the minerals iron, phosphorus, potassium and zinc, and vitamins B1, B3, B5 and B6.

Unique health benefits

The sulphated polysaccharides in sea vegetables are unique compounds called fucoidans[79]. Many studies show they have anti-inflammatory benefits as well as anti-viral properties[80]. Extracts from sea vegetables have an anti-thrombotic effect and can decrease the tendency of platelet cells to form clots. There is also on-going research into the anti-cancer properties of sea vegetables, particularly oestrogen-related cancers. As an excellent source of iodine they pay an important role in thyroid support.[81]

MUSHROOMS

Mushrooms are available to buy all year round. Ordinary white or brown mushrooms seem to contain the highest amounts of nutrients, though shitakii, oyster or any of the more exotic varieties are all good mushrooms to eat. Always buy mushrooms as fresh as possible. They should be firm, not spongy.

Mushrooms are an excellent source of phosphorus, copper, selenium and the vitamins B2 and B3. They are a very good source of potassium, zinc, manganese and vitamin B1 and a good source of vitamin B6, B12, folate, choline and protein.

Phytonutrients

Mushrooms contain the polysaccharide-like molecules beta-D-glucans and fucogalactans. They also contain conjugated linoleic acid (CLA), which is a unique type of fatty acid.

Unique health benefits

Mushrooms are known to help with the reduction of blood fat cells and to have antibiotic properties. Recent studies have shown that they have anti-cancer properties and their specific phytonutrients help to support the immune system and prevent inflammation.

ABOUT GABRIELA LERNER

I could say that I more or less grew up in my grandparents' vegetable garden in a small town in Germany. I used to love the fresh flavour of vegetables picked straight from the bush or out of the soil. Peas just didn't taste as good any more once my grandmother had cooked them to death.

Looking back at my life I can see many changes in my life. A move from Germany to England, bringing up two daughters, changing careers, starting businesses and moving on to new entrepreneurial adventures. But through all the changes, good, wholesome food always had a place in my life. I have a deep passion for food and love nothing more than seeing the happy, satisfied glow on the faces of people who eat what I have prepared.

In 1994 I was diagnosed with Fibromyalgia after 18 months of chronic pain, spending 5 out of 7 days in bed. Being diagnosed meant that I was able to manage my condition, to function and even work again. But I was never well and I always had to closely monitor how I used my energy, making it hard to have a social life on top of caring for young children and earning a living. I was on full-time medication, daily pain killers and I can't even imagine how worried my husband, Neil, and my family must have been. But one thing I knew was that Fibromyalgia doesn't kill, it's just very painful and limiting.

In 2011, following some routine check-ups, Neil was diagnosed with prostate cancer. This was a completely different ball game. Cancer kills. And it changed everything – to the better! Neil was determined to heal himself naturally and refused the conventional treat-ment he was offered. There is a whole story about what happened, but suffice to say that Neil and I decided to make some major lifestyle and nutrition changes. Through focussed and consistent steps we changed to eating a raw, plant-based, living, organic, nutrition-dense diet, reduced our workload and introduced exercise and relaxation. I started to see that our bodies have the amazing ability to heal themselves. Look at what happens when you cut yourself or break a bone. Perhaps you stop the bleeding or you have the bone set for it to grow together straight, but mostly the healing is done by the body. This principle is universal: given half a chance, the body will do its utmost to heal and be well. And this is what happened to me. Once I gave my body what it needed it started to heal. From there it was only a small step to combine my passion for wellness with my passion for food, and in particular raw, living food. I'm a trained Integrative Nutrition Health Coach, Raw Food Teacher and Raw Nutrition Coach. I'm always learning and developing. I love making food and I love supporting people in making a transition towards a healthier, more sustainable and happier life.

Gabriela Lerner AADP IAHC
Raw Nutrition Coach & Institute of Integrative Nutrition Health Coach
For more information please visit my website at **www.gabrielalerner.com**

Nothing is as powerful as action. Action immediately destroys procrastination, doubt and fear. Go for it, because now is the best time ever.

David Avocado Wolfe, 'Longevity Now'

THE MOVE TO MORE RAW FOOD

Making a commitment to live a healthier, more nutritious lifestyle can be overwhelming at first. But make small changes, one step at a time, and you will find not just your health improving, but your whole life and the lives of those near to you expanding. Gabriela would love to support you on your journey.

Blog & Recipes

Visit **www.gabrielalerner.com** for monthly blog posts on health, lifestyle and nutrition topics and new recipes. There you can also sign up to Gabriela's newsletter for monthly inspirational thoughts and news.

One-day Events

Experience a day of holistic, raw vegan living.
For more information visit www.gabrielalerner.com

Coaching

Coaching offers you hands-on guidance and support to fully embrace a holistic, raw vegan lifestyle. Gabriela offers online group programmes as well as private one-on-one coaching.
For more info visit **www.gabrielalerner.com**

Retreats

Whether you want to take your holistic, raw vegan lifestyle to the next level or just want a healthy break away from your busy life, join a weekend or week-long retreat. Gabriela runs events in the UK and it fantastic locations abroad.
For more information **www.gabrielalerner.com**

References from the Food Heroes section are available for download at
www.gabrielalerner.com/references

INDEX

Agar Agar
Cranberry Relish 113
Incan Chocolate Torte 80
Agave Syrup
Caramelised Onions 104
Age-related Macular Degeneration *125*
Alkalising *121*
Allium Family *129*
Allspice
Apple & Cranberry Oat Bar 77
Apple Crumble 73
Castara Sunset Noodles 48
Orange Cacao Torte 70
Walnut & Raisin Bread 101
Almonds *131*
Apple Crumble 73
Carrot & Ginger Pâté 43
Lime Pie 68
Mushroom And Basil Soup 32
Nut Or Seed Milk 114
Nut 'Roast' 62
Nut & Seed 'Parmesan' 111
Sprouted Lentil Hummus 37
The Perfect Salad 26
Amino Acids *131*
Anethole *122*
Antacid *127*
Anthocyanins *123*
Anti-Bacterial *123*
Anti-Cancer *120, 125, 130, 131, 132*
Anti-Fungal *123*
Anti-Inflammatory *121*
Anti-Microbial *123, 128, 129, 130*
Antioxidants *121, 125, 126, 127, 132*
Anti-thrombotic *133*
Apigenin *120, 130, 132*
Apple & Cranberry Oat Bar 77
Apple Crumble 73
Apples *126*
Apple & Cranberry Oat Bar 77
Apple Crumble 73
Super Green Smoothie 13

Walnut & Raisin Bread 101
Arthritis *120, 125, 130, 131, 133*
Asthma *126*
Avocados *126*
5-Minute Chop Bowl 27
Black Forest Cherry Tumbler 83
Fruit & Green Salad 23
Lime Pie 68
Nori Rolls 28
Orange Cacao Torte 70
Super Green Smoothie 13
The Perfect Salad 26
Ayurvedic Medicine *129*

Banana Breakfast Smoothie 17
Banana Ice Cream 75
Bananas *127*
Banana Breakfast Smoothie 17
Banana Ice Cream 75
Berry Berry Smoothie 13
Cacao Nib Oat Bars 72
Pineapple Kale Smoothie 12
Walnut & Raisin Bread 101
Basic Macadamia Nut Cheese 117
Basics 103
Basic Macadamia Nut Cheese 117
Caramelised Onions 104
Cashew Cream 115
Cashew Yoghurt 116
Cranberry Relish 113
Date & Mulberry Paste 105
Marinated Mushrooms 106
Nut Or Seed Milk 114
Nut & Seed 'Parmesan' 111
Pickled Ginger 118
Pine Nut 'Parmesan' Flakes 112
Raw Tomato Ketchup 107
Smoky Seeds 109
Spicy Curry Seeds 110
Sprouted buckwheat/buckwHeaties 108
Sprouting Nuts and Seeds 108
Basil, dried
Italian Seed Crackers 91
Basil, fresh
Beetroot & Courgette Roulade 60

Carrot Burgers 57
Castara Sunset Noodles 48
Courgette Ribbons With Smoky Tomato Sauce 58
Creamy Tomato And Red Pepper Soup 29
Kelp Noodles With Spinach Pesto 33
Mushroom And Basil Soup 32
Rawsagne 64
Thai Green Curry Kelp Noodles 56
The Perfect Salad 26
Bean Sprouts
Teriyaki Noodles 46
Beetroot
Beetroot & Courgette Roulade 60
Beetroot & Rosemary Crackers 92
Carrot & Beetroot Salad 41
Beetroot and Courgette Roulade 60
Beetroot & Rosemary Crackers 92
Berries *127*
Apple & Cranberry Oat Bar 77
Berry Berry Smoothie 13
Black Forest Cherry Tumbler 83
Cacao Goji Buckwheat Crunch 16
Courgette Ribbons With Smoky Tomato Sauce 58
Cranberry Relish 113
Date & Mulberry Paste 105
Fruit & Green Salad 23
Gooseberry Chia Mousse 84
Incan Chocolate Torte 80
Mulberry and Goji Chia Pudding 20
Nut 'Roast' 62
Rawsagne 64
Raw Tomato Ketchup 107
Stuffed Portobello Mushrooms With Sour Cream 51
Berry Berry Smoothie 13
Beta-carotene *120, 121, 122, 123, 125, 130*
Betaine *121*
Betalains *121*
Biotin *121, 123, 124, 125, 127, 131, 133*
Blackberries *127*
Berry Berry Smoothie 13
Lemon Mango Cheese Cake 87
Black Forest Cherry Tumbler 83
Blood Sugar *67, 72, 123, 126, 127, 128, 132*
Blood Vessels *120, 130, 132*

Blueberries *127*
Berry Berry Smoothie 13
Bok Choy
Super Green Smoothie 13
Bone Density *125*
Bowel *122, 127*
Brazil Nuts
Cacao Nib Oat Bars 72
English Breakfast 21
Incan Chocolate Torte 80
Nut Or Seed Milk 114
Orange Cacao Torte 70
Breads
Breads, Crackers & Wraps 89
Carrot & Onion Bread 97
Garlic Croutons 95
Walnut & Raisin Bread 101
Breads, Crackers & Wraps 89
Breakfast
Banana Breakfast Smoothie 17
Berry Berry Smoothie 13
Cacao Chia Pudding 18
Cacao Goji Buckwheat Crunch 16
Cashew Cream 115
Cashew Yoghurt 116
Cinnamon Buckwheat Crunch 15
English Breakfast 21
Fruit & Green Salad 23
Mulberry and Goji Chia Pudding 20
Nut Or Seed Milk 114
Pineapple Kale Smoothie 12
Super Green Smoothie 13
Tropical Green Smoothie 12
Break For Lunch 25
Broad Bean Pâté 36
Broad Beans
Broad Bean Pâté 36
Broccoli *120*
5-Minute Chop Bowl 27
Jewelled Broccoli Salad 34
Purple Sprouting Broccoli with Tarragon Cream 42
Bromelain *129*
Buckwheat *131*
Cacao Goji Buckwheat Crunch 16
Carrot & Onion Bread 97
Cinnamon Buckwheat Crunch 15
English Breakfast 21
Incan Chocolate Torte 80

Sprouted buckwheat/buckwHeaties 108
Stuffed Tomatoes With Cheesy Sauce 53
Walnut & Raisin Bread 101
Buckwheaties
Incan Chocolate Torte 80
Sprouted buckwheat/buckwHeaties 108

Cabbage *120*
5-Minute Chop Bowl 27
Carrot & Savoy Cabbage Salad 31
Castara Sunset Noodles 48
Hungarian Cabbage Salad 38
Spiced Red Cabbage 61
Cacao
Black Forest Cherry Tumbler 83
Cacao Chia Pudding 18
Cacao Goji Buckwheat Crunch 16
Incan Chocolate Torte 80
Orange Cacao Torte 70
Raw Rocky Road 82
Tahini Cacao Truffles 78
Cacao Chia Pudding 18
Cacao Goji Buckwheat Crunch 16
Cacao Nib Oat Bars 72
Cacao Nibs
Cacao Goji Buckwheat Crunch 16
Incan Chocolate Torte 80
Orange Cacao Torte 70
Caffeic Acid *125*
Cakes
Celebrate Sweet 67
Incan Chocolate Torte 80
Lemon Mango Cheese Cake 86
Lime Pie 68
Orange Cacao Torte 70
Calcium *120, 122, 124, 130, 131*
Cancer *120, 121, 122, 123, 124, 125, 127, 128, 130, 131, 133, 134*
Caramelised Onions 104
Caraway Seeds
Hungarian Cabbage Salad 38
Cardio-protective *122*
Cardiovascular *121, 122, 123, 124, 125, 126, 127, 129, 130, 131, 132, 133*
Carotenoids *120, 122, 125, 126, 128*
Carrot & Beetroot Salad 41
Carrot Burgers 57

Carrot & Ginger Pâté 43
Carrot & Onion Bread 97
Carrots *122*
Carrot & Beetroot Salad 41
Carrot Burgers 57
Carrot & Ginger Pâté 43
Carrot & Onion Bread 97
Carrot & Savoy Cabbage Salad 31
Castara Sunset Noodles 48
Nori Rolls 28
Sprouted Quinoa 'Tabbouleh' 39
Stuffed Tomatoes With Cheesy Sauce 53
Teriyaki Noodles 46
Thai Green Curry Kelp Noodles 56
Carrot & Savoy Cabbage Salad 31
Cashew Cream 115
Black Forest Cherry Tumbler 83
Cashew Nuts
Apple & Cranberry Oat Bar 77
Black Forest Cherry Tumbler 83
Cacao Nib Oat Bars 72
Cashew Cream 115
Cashew Yoghurt 116
Creamy Tomato And Red Pepper Soup 29
Gooseberry Chia Mousse 84
Incan Chocolate Torte 80
Lemon Mango Cheese Cake 86
Macadamia Lemon Biscuits 76
Purple Sprouting Broccoli with Tarragon Cream 42
Sour Cream 52
Stuffed Tomatoes With Cheesy Sauce 53
Thai Green Curry Kelp Noodles 56
Cashew Yoghurt 116
Castara Sunset Noodles 48
Catechins *126, 131*
Cauliflower
Cauliflower Rice 28
Nori Rolls 28
Cautions *120, 121, 122, 123, 124, 125, 126, 127, 128, 129*
Cayenne, ground
Castara Sunset Noodles 48
Green Corn Wraps 100
Mini Peppers With Nut Cheese 54
Spicy Curry Seeds 110
Celebrate Sweet 67

Celeriac
Beetroot & Courgette Roulade 60
Carrot Burgers 57

Celery *124*
Carrot Burgers 57
Carrot & Ginger Pâté 43
Fruit & Green Salad 23
Nut 'Roast' 62
Super Green Smoothie 13

Chard
Sprouted Quinoa 'Tabbouleh' 39
The Perfect Salad 26

Cheese
Basic Macadamia Nut Cheese 117
Lemon Mango 'Cheese' Cake 86
Nut & Seed 'Parmesan' 111
Pine Nut 'Parmesan' Flakes 112

Cherries
Black Forest Cherry Tumbler 83

Chia Seed Pizza Crust 98

Chia Seeds *131*
Apple Crumble 73
Banana Breakfast Smoothie 17
Cacao Chia Pudding 18
Cacao Goji Buckwheat Crunch 16
Carrot & Onion Bread 97
Chia Seed Pizza Crust 98
Gooseberry Chia Mousse 84
Italian Seed Crackers 91
Mulberry and Goji Chia Pudding 20
Walnut & Raisin Bread 101

Chillies
Thai Green Curry Kelp Noodles 56

Chilli, ground
Smoky Seeds 109

Chives
Sour Cream 52

Chlorella
Super Green Smoothie 13

Chlorogenic Acid *131*

Cholesterol *121, 122, 128, 131, 132, 133*

Chromium *120, 125*

Cinnamon
Apple & Cranberry Oat Bar 77
Apple Crumble 73
Banana Breakfast Smoothie 17
Castara Sunset Noodles 48
Cinnamon Buckwheat Crunch 15

Orange Cacao Torte 70
Walnut & Raisin Bread 101

Cinnamon Buckwheat Crunch 15
Black Forest Cherry Tumbler 83
Raw Rocky Road 82

Circulation *120, 130, 132*

Cloves
Banana Breakfast Smoothie 17
Spiced Red Cabbage 61

Coconut, desiccated
Lime Pie 68
Orange Cacao Torte 70
Raw Rocky Road 82

Coconut Nectar
Black Forest Cherry Tumbler 83
Caramelised Onions 104
Gooseberry Chia Mousse 84
Incan Chocolate Torte 80
Lemon Mango Cheese Cake 86
Lime Pie 68
Orange Cacao Torte 70
Tahini Cacao Truffles 78

Coconut Oil
Cacao Nib Oat Bars 72
Incan Chocolate Torte 80
Lemon Mango Cheese Cake 86
Lime Pie 68
Mulberry and Goji Chia Pudding 20
Orange Cacao Torte 70
Raw Rocky Road 82
Thai Green Curry Kelp Noodles 56

Coconut Sugar
Caramelised Onions 104
Pickled Ginger 118
Raw Rocky Road 82

Coconut Water
Thai Green Curry Kelp Noodles 56
Tropical Green Smoothie 12

Cognitive Function *127*

Condiments
Cranberry Relish 113
Pickled Ginger 118
Raw Tomato Ketchup 107

Constipation *127*

Copper *120, 121, 122, 123, 124, 125, 126, 127, 128, 129, 130, 131, 132, 133*

Coriander, fresh *129*
Carrot & Beetroot Salad 41

Carrot & Ginger Pâté 43
Castara Sunset Noodles 48
Sprouted Quinoa 'Tabbouleh' 39
Thai Green Curry Kelp Noodles 56

Coriander, ground
Carrot & Savoy Cabbage Salad 31
Green Corn Wraps 100
Moroccan Seed Crackers 90

Corn
Green Corn Wraps 100

Courgette Ribbons With Smoky Tomato Sauce 58

Courgettes
Beetroot & Courgette Roulade 60
Chia Seed Pizza Crust 98
Courgette Ribbons With Smoky Tomato Sauce 58
Green Corn Wraps 100
Jewelled Broccoli Salad 34
Rawsagne 64
Teriyaki Noodles 46

Courmarins *124*

Crackers
Beetroot & Rosemary Crackers 92
Breads, Crackers & Wraps 89
Chia Seed Pizza Crust 98
Italian Seed Crackers 91
Moroccan Seed Crackers 90
Yellow Pepper & Saffron Crackers 94

Cranberries
Apple & Cranberry Oat Bar 77
Berry Berry Smoothie 13
Cranberry Relish 113

Cranberry Relish 113

Cream
Cashew Cream 115

Creamy Tomato And Red Pepper Soup 29

Cruciferous *121*

Cucumber *124*
Super Green Smoothie 13

Cumin, ground
Moroccan Seed Crackers 90
Smoky Seeds 109
Sprouted Lentil Hummus 37

Curcumin *131*

Curry
Spicy Curry Seeds 110

Cystic Fibrosis *131*

Date & Mulberry Paste 105
Caramelised Onions 104
Carrot & Beetroot Salad 41
Carrot & Onion Bread 97
Macadamia Lemon Biscuits 76
Nori Rolls 28
Stuffed Tomatoes With Cheesy Sauce 53

Dates
Apple & Cranberry Oat Bar 77
Apple Crumble 73
Beetroot & Courgette Roulade 60
Carrot & Onion Bread 97
Castara Sunset Noodles 48
Creamy Tomato And Red Pepper Soup 29
Date & Mulberry Paste 105
Incan Chocolate Torte 80
Lemon Mango Cheese Cake 86
Lime Pie 68
Macadamia Lemon Biscuits 76
Orange Cacao Torte 70
Raw Tomato Ketchup 107

Dehydrated Foods
Apple & Cranberry Oat Bar 77
Beetroot & Rosemary Crackers 92
Breads, Crackers & Wraps 89
Caramelised Onions 104
Carrot Burgers 57
Carrot & Onion Bread 97
Chia Seed Pizza Crust 98
Garlic Croutons 95
Green Corn Wraps 100
Italian Seed Crackers 91
Marinated Mushrooms 106
Moroccan Seed Crackers 90
Mushroom Steaks 49
Pine Nut 'Parmesan' Flakes 112
Rawsagne 64
Raw Tomato Ketchup 107
Smoky Seeds 109
Spicy Curry Seeds 110
Sprouted buckwheat/buckwHeaties 108
Walnut & Raisin Bread 101
Yellow Pepper & Saffron Crackers 94

Desserts
Apple Crumble 73
Banana Ice Cream 75
Black Forest Cherry Tumbler 83
Cacao Chia Pudding 18
Celebrate Sweet 67
Gooseberry Chia Mousse 84
Incan Chocolate Torte 80

Lemon Mango Cheese Cake 86
Lime Pie 68
Mulberry and Goji Chia Pudding 20
Orange Cacao Torte 70
Detoxification *120*, *122, 123*
Detoxifier *129*
Diabetics *123*
Dips
Sprouted Lentil Hummus 37
Dressings
Beetroot & Courgette Roulade 60
Jewelled Broccoli Salad 34
Purple Sprouting Broccoli with
Tarragon Cream 42
Teriyaki Noodles 46
Basic Dressing 26
Almond Butter Dressing 26
Avocado Basil Dressing 26
Dulce *133*
English Breakfast 21
The Perfect Salad 26

Electrolyte *124*
English Breakfast 21
Enzymes *8, 121, 122, 126, 127, 128, 131, 133*
Equipment 9
Eye Health *122*
Eyes *127*

Fatty Alcohols *126*
Fennel *122*
Castara Sunset Noodles 48
Teriyaki Noodles 46
Fibre *105, 120, 121, 122, 123, 124, 125, 126, 127, 128, 129, 131, 132*
Five-MInute Chop Bowl 27
Flavanols *128*
Flavonoids *120, 123, 124, 125, 126, 127, 128, 129, 131, 132*
Flavonones *125*
Flax Seeds *132*
Beetroot & Rosemary Crackers 92
Carrot & Onion Bread 97
Chia Seed Pizza Crust 98
Garlic Croutons 95
Green Corn Wraps 100

Italian Seed Crackers 91
Macadamia Lemon Biscuits 76
Moroccan Seed Crackers 90
Mulberry and Goji Chia Pudding 20
Nut & Seed 'Parmesan' 111
Walnut & Raisin Bread 101
Yellow Pepper & Saffron Crackers 94
Folate *120, 121, 122, 123, 124, 125, 126, 127, 128, 129, 130, 131, 132*
Folic Acid *120, 121, 122*
Fruit & Green Salad 23

Gabriela Lerner 134
Gall Bladder *121, 123, 127, 130*
Garam Massala
Spicy Curry Seeds 110
Garlic *129*
Broad Bean Pâté 36
Castara Sunset Noodles 48
Chia Seed Pizza Crust 98
Garlic Croutons 95
Green Corn Wraps 100
Italian Seed Crackers 91
Kelp Noodles With Spinach Pesto 33
Moroccan Seed Crackers 90
Mushroom And Basil Soup 32
Mushroom Steaks 49
Rawsagne 64
Sprouted Lentil Hummus 37
Teriyaki Noodles 46
Thai Green Curry Kelp Noodles 56
Garlic Croutons 95
Garlic, powder
Mini Peppers With Nut Cheese 54
Nut & Seed 'Parmesan' 111
Raw Tomato Ketchup 107
Spicy Curry Seeds 110
Giardia Infections *128*
Ginger, fresh *130*
Carrot & Beetroot Salad 41
Carrot & Ginger Pâté 43
Castara Sunset Noodles 48
Jewelled Broccoli Salad 34
Pickled Ginger 118
Teriyaki Noodles 46
Thai Green Curry Kelp Noodles 56
Ginger, ground
Moroccan Seed Crackers 90

Gingerol *120, 130, 132*

Ginger, pickled 118
Teriyaki Noodles 46

Glucosinolates *120, 125, 130, 131, 133*

Goji Berries
Cacao Goji Buckwheat Crunch 16
Courgette Ribbons With Smoky Tomato Sauce 58
Mulberry and Goji Chia Pudding 20
Nut 'Roast' 62
Rawsagne 64
Stuffed Portobello Mushrooms With Sour Cream 51

Golden Berries
Incan Chocolate Torte 80
Raw Tomato Ketchup 107

Gooseberries
Gooseberry Chia Mousse 84

Gooseberry Chia Mousse 84

Gout *124*

Grapes *127*
Carrot & Savoy Cabbage Salad 31

Green Corn Wraps 100

Greens
The Perfect Salad 26

Green Tea
Super Green Smoothie 13

Gut *122, 123, 124, 127*

Hazelnuts *132*
Banana Breakfast Smoothie 17
Cacao Chia Pudding 18
Garlic Croutons 95
Incan Chocolate Torte 80
Lime Pie 68
Mulberry and Goji Chia Pudding 20
Nut Or Seed Milk 114
Tahini Cacao Truffles 78

Heavy Metal *123, 129*

Hemp Oil
Beetroot & Courgette Roulade 60

Hemp Powder
Mulberry and Goji Chia Pudding 20

Hemp Seeds *132*
5-Minute Chop Bowl 27
Apple & Cranberry Oat Bar 77
Cacao Chia Pudding 18
Nori Rolls 28
Nut Or Seed Milk 114

The Perfect Salad 26

Herbs
Broad Bean Pâté 36
Carrot Burgers 57
Carrot & Ginger Pâté 43
Castara Sunset Noodles 48
Creamy Tomato And Red Pepper Soup 29
Herbs & Spices *129*
Kelp Noodles With Spinach Pesto 33
Mini Peppers With Nut Cheese 54
Mushroom And Basil Soup 32
Mushroom Steaks 49
Nut 'Roast' 62
Purple Sprouting Broccoli with
Tarragon Cream 42
Rawsagne 64
Sour Cream 52
Sprouted Lentil Hummus 37
Sprouted Quinoa 'Tabbouleh' 39
Stuffed Portobello Mushrooms With Sour Cream 51
The Perfect Salad 26

Herbs de Provence
Nut 'Roast' 62

Herbs, dried
Courgette Ribbons With Smoky Tomato Sauce 58

Herbs & Spices *129*

Hijiki *133*
Teriyaki Noodles 46
Thai Green Curry Kelp Noodles 56

Hummus
Sprouted Lentil Hummus 37

Hungarian Cabbage Salad 38

Hydroxycinnamic Acids *125*

Ice Creams
Banana Ice Cream 75

Incan Chocolate Torte 80

Inflammation *120, 122, 123, 124, 129, 130*

Insulin Metabolism *123*

Insulin Resistance *132*

Iodine *127, 133*

Iron *120, 125, 130, 132, 133*

Italian Herbs, dried
Garlic Croutons 95

Italian Seed Crackers 91

Jewelled Broccoli Salad 34

Juglone *101, 133*

Kaempferol Glycosides *122*

Kaempherol *128*

Kale *120*
5-Minute Chop Bowl 27
Pineapple Kale Smoothie 12
The Perfect Salad 26

Kelp *133*
Chia Seed Pizza Crust 98
Kelp Noodles With Spinach Pesto 33
Thai Green Curry Kelp Noodles 56

Kelp Noodles With Spinach Pesto 33

Ketchup
Raw Tomato Ketchup 107

Kidney *121, 123, 127, 130*

Latex Allergy *126, 127*

Leafy Greens *120*
Broccoli *120*
Cabbage *120*
Kale *120*
Romaine Lettuce *120*

Lemon Grass
Thai Green Curry Kelp Noodles 56

Lemon Mango Cheese Cake 86

Lemons *128*
5-Minute Chop Bowl 27
Banana Ice Cream 75
Basic Macadamia Nut Cheese 117
Beetroot & Rosemary Crackers 92
Broad Bean Pâté 36
Cacao Nib Oat Bars 72
Carrot & Beetroot Salad 41
Castara Sunset Noodles 48
English Breakfast 21
Fruit & Green Salad 23
Gooseberry Chia Mousse 84
Incan Chocolate Torte 80
Jewelled Broccoli Salad 34
Lemon Mango Cheese Cake 86
Marinated Mushrooms 106
Mini Peppers With Nut Cheese 54
Mushroom And Basil Soup 32
Mushroom Steaks 49
Nori Rolls 28
Orange Cacao Torte 70

Pineapple Kale Smoothie 12
Pine Nut 'Parmesan' Flakes 112
Purple Sprouting Broccoli with
Tarragon Cream 42
Raw Tomato Ketchup 107
Sprouted Lentil Hummus 37
Stuffed Portobello Mushrooms WIth Sour Cream 51
Stuffed Tomatoes With Cheesy Sauce 53
Super Green Smoothie 13
The Perfect Salad 26
Tropical Green Smoothie 12

Lemons, preserved
Carrot Burgers 57
Purple Sprouting Broccoli with
Tarragon Cream 42

Lentils
5-Minute Chop Bowl 27
Sprouted Lentil Hummus 37

Lettuce
The Perfect Salad 26

Lignans *122, 124*

Lime Pie 68

Limes *128*
Castara Sunset Noodles 48
Lime Pie 68
Thai Green Curry Kelp Noodles 56
The Perfect Salad 26
Yellow Pepper & Saffron Crackers 94

Limonene *120, 130, 132*

Limonin *128*

Linseeds *132*
Beetroot & Rosemary Crackers 92
Carrot & Onion Bread 97
Chia Seed Pizza Crust 98
Garlic Croutons 95
Green Corn Wraps 100
Italian Seed Crackers 91
Macadamia Lemon Biscuits 76
Moroccan Seed Crackers 90
Mulberry and Goji Chia Pudding 20
Nut & Seed 'Parmesan' 111
Walnut & Raisin Bread 101
Yellow Pepper & Saffron Crackers 94

Liver *120, 125, 130, 131, 133*

Longevity *128*

Lucuma Powder
Apple Crumble 73
Gooseberry Chia Mousse 84

Tahini Cacao Truffles 78

Lunch
Break For Lunch 25
Fruit & Green Salad 23

Lutein *121*

Luteolin *120, 130, 132*

Lycopene *125*

Macadamia Lemon Biscuits 76

Macadamia Nuts
Basic Macadamia Nut Cheese 117
Carrot Burgers 57
Kelp Noodles With Spinach Pesto 33
Mini Peppers With Nut Cheese 54
Nori Rolls 28
Purple Sprouting Broccoli with
Tarragon Cream 42
Raw Rocky Road 82

Maca Powder
Apple Crumble 73
Banana Breakfast Smoothie 17
Black Forest Cherry Tumbler 83
Cacao Chia Pudding 18
Cacao Goji Buckwheat Crunch 16
Cacao Nib Oat Bars 72
Cinnamon Buckwheat Crunch 15
Mulberry and Goji Chia Pudding 20
Raw Rocky Road 82
Tahini Cacao Truffles 78

Magnesium *120, 121, 122, 124, 125, 128, 130, 131, 132*

Manganese *120, 125, 130, 131, 133*

Mangos *128*
Fruit & Green Salad 23
Lemon Mango Cheese Cake 86
Tropical Green Smoothie 12

Marinated Mushrooms 106

Meet To Eat 45

Memory *127, 130*

Methylation Pathways *122, 124*

Mini Peppers With Nut Cheese 54

Mint, fresh
Sprouted Quinoa 'Tabbouleh' 39

Miso
Carrot Burgers 57
Carrot & Ginger Pâté 43

Sprouted Lentil Hummus 37
Sprouted Quinoa 'Tabbouleh' 39

Mixed herbs, dried
Rawsagne 64

Mixed Spice
Cacao Nib Oat Bars 72

Molybdenum *121, 122, 124, 125, 131, 133*

Monounsaturated Fats *131*

Moroccan Seed Crackers 90

Mulberries
Carrot & Onion Bread 97
Date & Mulberry Paste 105
Incan Chocolate Torte 80
Macadamia Lemon Biscuits 76
Mulberry and Goji Chia Pudding 20

Mulberry and Goji Chia Pudding 20

Mushroom And Basil Soup 32

Mushrooms *133*
Marinated Mushrooms 106
Mushroom And Basil Soup 32
Mushroom Steaks 49
Nori Rolls 28
Nut 'Roast' 62
Rawsagne 64
Stuffed Portobello Mushrooms WIth Sour Cream 51
The Perfect Salad 26

Mushroom Steaks 49

Myristicin *120, 130, 132*

Nausea *120, 130, 132*

Nerve Cells *127*

Neurogenerative Disorders *127*

Nightshade Family *125*

Noodles
Castara Sunset Noodles 48
Courgette Ribbons With Smoky Tomato Sauce 58
Kelp Noodles With Spinach Pesto 33
Teriyaki Noodles 46
Thai Green Curry Kelp Noodles 56

Nori *133*
Moroccan Seed Crackers 90
Nori Rolls 28
Spicy Nori Bites 55
The Perfect Salad 26

Nori Rolls 28

Nut Cheeses
Basic Macadamia Nut Cheese 117
Mini Peppers With Nut Cheese 54

Nut Or Seed Milk 114

Nutritional Yeast
Basic Macadamia Nut Cheese 117
Broad Bean Pâté 36
Garlic Croutons 95
Kelp Noodles With Spinach Pesto 33
Mini Peppers With Nut Cheese 54
Nut & Seed 'Parmesan' 111
Purple Sprouting Broccoli with
Tarragon Cream 42
Stuffed Tomatoes With Cheesy Sauce 53

Nut 'Roast' 62

Nut & Seed 'Parmesan' 111

Nuts & Seeds *131*

Oats, rolled
Apple & Cranberry Oat Bar 77
Apple Crumble 73
Cacao Nib Oat Bars 72

Obesity *132*

Olive Oil
5-Minute Chop Bowl 27
Broad Bean Pâté 36
Caramelised Onions 104
Carrot & Beetroot Salad 41
Carrot & Savoy Cabbage Salad 31
Courgette Ribbons With Smoky Tomato Sauce 58
Cranberry Relish 113
Creamy Tomato And Red Pepper Soup 29
English Breakfast 21
Garlic Croutons 95
Green Corn Wraps 100
Kelp Noodles With Spinach Pesto 33
Marinated Mushrooms 106
Mini Peppers With Nut Cheese 54
Mushroom Steaks 49
Nut 'Roast' 62
Pine Nut 'Parmesan' Flakes 112
Purple Sprouting Broccoli with
Tarragon Cream 42
Rawsagne 64
Spiced Red Cabbage 61
Sprouted Lentil Hummus 37
Sprouted Quinoa 'Tabbouleh' 39
Stuffed Portobello Mushrooms WIth Sour Cream 51
The Perfect Salad 26

Olives
Purple Sprouting Broccoli with
Tarragon Cream 42
Rawsagne 64

Omega 3 Fatty Acids *120, 125, 126, 130, 131, 133*

Omega 6 Fatty Acids *132, 133*

Onion, powder
Courgette Ribbons With Smoky Tomato Sauce 58
Spiced Red Cabbage 61

Onions
Beetroot & Rosemary Crackers 92
Caramelised Onions 104
Carrot & Ginger Pâté 43
Carrot & Onion Bread 97
Castara Sunset Noodles 48
Chia Seed Pizza Crust 98
Cranberry Relish 113
Mini Peppers With Nut Cheese 54
Onion *123*
Sprouted Quinoa 'Tabbouleh' 39

Onions, powder
Rawsagne 64

Orange Cacao Torte 70

Oranges
Berry Berry Smoothie 13
Carrot & Ginger Pâté 43
Orange Cacao Torte 70
Tropical Green Smoothie 12

Oregano, dried
Italian Seed Crackers 91

Organic *31, 37, 122, 124, 126, 127, 128, 133, 134*

Osteoarthritis *126*

Oxalates *121, 123, 127*

Oxidative Stress *120, 130, 132*

Papayas
Castara Sunset Noodles 48

Paprika
Courgette Ribbons With Smoky Tomato Sauce 58
Raw Tomato Ketchup 107
Smoky Seeds 109

Parmesan
Nut & Seed 'Parmesan' Flakes 111

Parsley *130*
Beetroot & Courgette Roulade 60
Broad Bean Pâté 36
Carrot Burgers 57

Chia Seed Pizza Crust 98
Marinated Mushrooms 106
Mini Peppers With Nut Cheese 54
Mushroom Steaks 49
Nut 'Roast' 62
Sour Cream 52
Sprouted Lentil Hummus 37
Stuffed Portobello Mushrooms WIth Sour Cream 51

Parsnips
Castara Sunset Noodles 48
Nori Rolls 28

Pâtés
Broad Bean Pâté 36
Carrot & Ginger Pâté 43
Sprouted Lentil Hummus 37

Pears
Fruit & Green Salad 23
PIneapple Kale Smoothie 12

Peas
Sprouted Quinoa 'Tabbouleh' 39
Thai Green Curry Kelp Noodles 56

Pecan Nuts
Apple & Cranberry Oat Bar 77
Apple Crumble 73
Kelp Noodles With Spinach Pesto 33
Lemon Mango Cheese Cake 86
Nut 'Roast' 62
Rawsagne 64
Stuffed Tomatoes With Cheesy Sauce 53

Pectin *126*

Peppers *125*
5-Minute Chop Bowl 27
Creamy Tomato And Red Pepper Soup 29
Mini Peppers With Nut Cheese 54
Thai Green Curry Kelp Noodles 56
Yellow Pepper & Saffron Crackers 94

Pesticides *8, 127, 128*

Phenolic Acid *129*

Phosphorous *120, 121, 122, 123, 124, 125, 126, 127, 128, 129, 130, 132*

Phytonutrients *8, 120, 122, 123, 125, 126, 127, 129, 131, 132, 133*

Phytosterol *126, 132*

Phytosterols *132*

Pickled Ginger 118

Pickles
Pickled Ginger 118

Pies
Lime Pie 68

Pineapple *129*
Pineapple Kale Smoothie 12
Tropical Green Smoothie 12

Pineapple Kale Smoothie *12*

Pine Nut 'Parmesan' Flakes 112

Pine Nuts
Broad Bean Pâté 36
Mini Peppers With Nut Cheese 54
Nori Rolls 28
Pine Nut 'Parmesan' Flakes 112

Pizza
Chia Seed Pizza Crust 98

Poison Ivy 129

Polyhydroxylated Fatty Acids *126*

Polyphenols *120, 123, 128, 129*

Polysaccharides *122, 124*

Pomegranates *129*
Cranberry Relish 113
Fruit & Green Salad 23
Jewelled Broccoli Salad 34

Potassium *61, 121, 122, 123, 124, 125, 126, 127, 128, 130, 131, 133*

Pre-Biotic *122, 127*

Proanthocyanidins *132*

Pro-Biotics
Basic Macadamia Nut Cheese 117
Cashew Yoghurt 116
Lemon Mango Cheese Cake 86
Pine Nut 'Parmesan' Flakes 112

Protein *8, 16, 18, 20, 26, 29, 36, 37, 120, 123, 131, 132*

Pro-vitamin A *120, 129*

Psyllium Husks
Carrot & Onion Bread 97
Garlic Croutons 95
Walnut & Raisin Bread 101

Pterostilbene *127*

Pthalides *124*

Pudding
Cacao Chia Pudding 18

Pumpkin Seed Oil
Jewelled Broccoli Salad 34

Pumpkin Seeds *132*
Cacao Chia Pudding 18
Cacao Goji Buckwheat Crunch 16
Chia Seed Pizza Crust 98
Cinnamon Buckwheat Crunch 15
Moroccan Seed Crackers 90
Smoky Seeds 109
Spicy Curry Seeds 110
The Perfect Salad 26
Walnut & Raisin Bread 101

Purple Sprouting Broccoli with Tarragon Cream 42

Quercetin *120, 122, 123, 124, 125, 126, 128, 129, 132*

Quinoa
Sprouted Quinoa 'Tabbouleh' 39
Stuffed Portobello Mushrooms With Sour Cream 51

Quinone *133*

Raisins *127*
Apple Crumble 73
Carrot & Ginger Pâté 43
Spiced Red Cabbage 61
Sprouted Quinoa 'Tabbouleh' 39
Walnut & Raisin Bread 101

Raspberries *127*
Black Forest Cherry Tumbler 83
Cacao Goji Buckwheat Crunch 16
Lemon Mango Cheese Cake 86
Orange Cacao Torte 71

Raw Food
Why Raw Food 8

Raw Rocky Road 82

Rawsagne *64*

Raw Tomato Ketchup 107

Resveratrol *127, 128*

Rheumatoid Arthritis *126*

Romaine Lettuce *120*
Berry Berry Smoothie 13

Roots & Bulbs
Carrots *122*
Fennel *122*
Onion *123*
Sweet Potato *123*

Rosemary
Beetroot & Rosemary Crackers 92

Rowena Paxton *135*

Rutin *94, 122, 131*

Saffron
Yellow Pepper & Saffron Crackers 94

Salads
5-Minute Chop Bowl 27
Carrot & Beetroot Salad 41
Carrot & Savoy Cabbage Salad 31
Fruit & Green Salad 23
Hungarian Cabbage Salad 38
Jewelled Broccoli Salad 34
Purple Sprouting Broccoli with Tarragon Cream 42
Spiced Red Cabbage 61
Sprouted Quinoa 'Tabbouleh' 39
The Perfect Salad 26

Salmonella *129*

Sauces
Raw Tomato Ketchup 107
Smoky Tomato Sauce 58
Thai Green Curry Sauce 56

Seagreens *133*

Seaweeds *133*
Moroccan Seed Crackers 90
Nori Rolls 28
Teriyaki Noodles 46
Thai Green Curry Kelp Noodles 56
The Perfect Salad 26

Selenium *120, 130, 132*

Sesame Oil
Carrot & Beetroot Salad 41
Castara Sunset Noodles 48
Teriyaki Noodles 46

Sesame Seeds
Beetroot & Courgette Roulade 60
Carrot & Beetroot Salad 41
Carrot & Onion Bread 97
Carrot & Savoy Cabbage Salad 31
Castara Sunset Noodles 48
Chia Seed Pizza Crust 98
Italian Seed Crackers 91
Moroccan Seed Crackers 90
Nut Or Seed Milk 114
Smoky Seeds 109
Sprouted Lentil Hummus 37
Sprouted Quinoa 'Tabbouleh' 39
Stuffed Portobello Mushrooms With Sour Cream 51
Yellow Pepper & Saffron Crackers 94

Smoked Paprika, ground
Smoky Seeds 109

Smoky Seeds 109

Smoothies
Banana Breakfast Smoothie 17
Berry Berry Smothie 13
Pineapple Kale Smoothie 12
Super Green Smoothie 13
Tropical Green Smoothie 12

Snacks
Apple & Cranberry Oat Bar 77
Cacao Goji Buckwheat Crunch 16
Cacao Nib Oat Bars 72
Macadamia Lemon Biscuits 76

Soups
Creamy Tomato And Red Pepper Soup 29
Mushroom And Basil Soup 32

Sour Cream 52

Spiced Red Cabbage 61

Spicy Curry Seeds 110

Spicy Nori Bites 55

Spinach
English Breakfast 21
Fruit & Green Salad 23
Green Corn Wraps 100
Kelp Noodles With Spinach Pesto 33
Rawsagne 64
Stuffed Tomatoes With Cheesy Sauce 53
The Perfect Salad 26
Tropical Green Smoothie 12

Spiralising
Castara Sunset Noodles 48
Teriyaki Noodles 46

Spirulina
Super Green Smoothie 13

Sprouted buckwheat/buckwHeaties 108

Sprouted Lentil Hummus 37

Sprouted Quinoa 'Tabbouleh' 39

Sprouting
5-Minute Chop Bowl 27
Carrot & Onion Bread 97
Sprouted buckwheat/buckwHeaties 108
Sprouted Lentil Hummus 37
Sprouting Seeds and Nuts 108
Stuffed Tomatoes With Cheesy Sauce 53
Teriyaki Noodles 46
Walnut & Raisin Bread 101

Starters
Mini Peppers With Nut Cheese 54
Spicy Nori Bites 55

Start The Day 11

Strawberries *127*
Black Forest Cherry Tumbler *83*
Fruit & Green Salad 23
Gooseberry Chia Mousse *84*
Jewelled Broccoli Salad 34

Stuffed Portobello Mushrooms With Herb Sour Cream 51

Stuffed Tomatoes With Cheesy Sauce 53

Stuffing
Mini Peppers With Nut Cheese 54
Stuffed Portobello Mushrooms With Sour Cream 51
Stuffed Tomatoes With Cheesy Sauce 53

Sulphides *123*

Sunflower Seeds *132*
Apple Crumble 73
Beetroot & Rosemary Crackers 92
Cacao Goji Buckwheat Crunch 16
Cacao Nib Oat Bars 72
Carrot Burgers 57
Carrot & Ginger Pâté 43
Carrot & Onion Bread 97
Chia Seed Pizza Crust 98
Cinnamon Buckwheat Crunch 15
English Breakfast 21
Italian Seed Crackers 91
Lemon Mango Cheese Cake 86
Lime Pie 68
Moroccan Seed Crackers 90
Nut Or Seed Milk 114
Nut 'Roast' 62
Nut & Seed 'Parmesan' 111
Orange Cacao Torte 70
Purple Sprouting Broccoli with Tarragon Cream 42
Smoky Seeds 109
Spicy Curry Seeds 110
Stuffed Tomatoes With Cheesy Sauce 53
The Perfect Salad 26
Walnut & Raisin Bread 101
Yellow Pepper & Saffron Crackers 94

Sunflower Shoots
Nori Rolls 28

Super Green Smoothie 13

Sweetcorn
Green Corn Wraps 100
Thai Green Curry Kelp Noodles 56

Sweet Potatoes 123
Castara Sunset Noodles 48

Sweets
Apple & Cranberry Oat Bar 77
Apple Crumble 73
Banana Ice Cream 75
Black Forest Cherry Tumbler 83
Cacao Chia Pudding 18
Cacao Nib Oat Bars 72
Cashew Cream 115
Celebrate Sweet 67
Gooseberry Chia Mousse 84
Incan Chocolate Torte 80
Lemon Mango Cheese Cake 86
Lime Pie 68
Macadamia Lemon Biscuits 76
Mulberry and Goji Chia Pudding 20
Orange Cacao Torte 70
Tahini Cacao Truffles 78

Swiss Chard
Sprouted Quinoa 'Tabbouleh' 39

Tahini
Beetroot & Courgette Roulade 60
Sprouted Lentil Hummus 37
Tahini Cacao Truffles 78

Tahini Cacao Truffles 78

Tamari
Beetroot & Courgette Roulade 60
Caramelised Onions 104
Carrot & Beetroot Salad 41
Carrot & Onion Bread 97
Castara Sunset Noodles 48
Marinated Mushrooms 106
Moroccan Seed Crackers 90
Mushroom And Basil Soup 32
Nut 'Roast' 62
Purple Sprouting Broccoli with Tarragon Cream 42
Smoky Seeds 109
Stuffed Portobello Mushrooms With Sour Cream 51
Teriyaki Noodles 46
Thai Green Curry Kelp Noodles 56
The Perfect Salad 26

Tamari Seeds
Spicy Curry Seeds 110

Tannins *101, 127, 133*

Tarragon, fresh
Purple Sprouting Broccoli with
Tarragon Cream 42

Teriyaki Noodles 46

Thai
Thai Green Curry Kelp Noodles 56

Thai Green Curry
Thai Green Curry Kelp Noodles 56

Thai Green Curry Kelp Noodles 56

The Move to More Raw Food 136

The Perfect Salad 26

Thyroid *120, 125, 130, 131, 133*

Tomatoes *125*
Courgette Ribbons With Smoky Tomato Sauce 58
Creamy Tomato And Red Pepper Soup 29
Italian Seed Crackers 91
Nut 'Roast' 62
Rawsagne 64
Raw Tomato Ketchup 107
Spicy Nori Bites 55
Sprouted Quinoa 'Tabbouleh' 39
Stuffed Tomatoes With Cheesy Sauce 53
The Perfect Salad 26

Tomatoes, sun-dried
Courgette Ribbons With Smoky Tomato Sauce 58
Creamy Tomato And Red Pepper Soup 29
Nut 'Roast' 62
Rawsagne 64
Raw Tomato Ketchup 107
Stuffed Portobello Mushrooms With Sour Cream 51
Stuffed Tomatoes With Cheesy Sauce 53

Tropical Green Smoothie 12

Tumours *120, 130, 132*

Turmeric *131*
Cacao Chia Pudding 18
English Breakfast 21

Turmeric, fresh
Castara Sunset Noodles 48

Turmeric, ground
Pine Nut 'Parmesan' Flakes 112

Type 2 Diabetes *132*

Vanilla
Banana Ice Cream 75
Black Forest Cherry Tumbler 83
Gooseberry Chia Mousse 84

Incan Chocolate Torte 80
Lemon Mango Cheese Cake 86
Lime Pie 68
Orange Cacao Torte 70
Raw Rocky Road 82
Tahini Cacao Truffles 78

Vinegar, cider
Beetroot & Courgette Roulade 60
Carrot & Beetroot Salad 41
Castara Sunset Noodles 48
Hungarian Cabbage Salad 38
Kelp Noodles With Spinach Pesto 33
Nori Rolls 28
Pickled Ginger 118
Spiced Red Cabbage 61
Sprouted Lentil Hummus 37
Sprouted Quinoa 'Tabbouleh' 39
Stuffed Tomatoes With Cheesy Sauce 53
The Perfect Salad 26

Vinegar, rice
Teriyaki Noodles 46

Viruses *128*

Vitamin A *122, 123*

Vitamin Bs *120, 125, 130, 131, 133*

Vitamin C *121*

Vitamin E *101, 133*

Vitamin K *121, 122, 124, 127, 128, 129*

Vitamins *8, 105, 120, 121, 122, 123, 124, 125, 126, 128, 129, 130, 131, 132*

Vitamins C *120, 121, 125*

Volatile Oils *120, 130, 132*

Vomiting *120, 130, 132*

Wakame *133*

Walnut & Raisin Bread 101

Walnuts *133*
Courgette Ribbons With Smoky Tomato Sauce 58
Incan Chocolate Torte 80
Jewelled Broccoli Salad 34
Nut & Seed 'Parmesan' 111
Stuffed Portobello Mushrooms With Sour Cream 51
Tahini Cacao Truffles 78
Walnut & Raisin Bread 101

Warts *120, 130, 132*

Watercress *121*
Nori Rolls 28
The Perfect Salad 26

Wraps
Breads, Crackers & Wraps 89
Green Corn Wraps 100

Yeast Infections *129*

Yellow Pepper & Saffron Crackers 94

Zeaxanthin *121*

Zinc *120, 125, 130, 131, 133*